How to Publish Your Book on CreateSpace and Kindle

Easy Publishing with Word 2007, 2010, 2013 & 2016

by Russ Crowley

Published by Russ Crowley

How to Publish Your Book on CreateSpace and Kindle

http://www.russcrowley.com

ISBN: 978-1501014628

Disclaimer

While every effort has been made by the author to present accurate and up-to-date information within this book, it is apparent technologies rapidly change; and, therefore, the author reserves the right to update the contents and information provided herein as these changes progress. The author takes no responsibility for any errors or omissions if such discrepancies exist within this document.

Any results obtained by readers following the instruction in this book will vary based on skill level and individual perception of the contents herein, and thus no guarantees, monetarily or otherwise, can be made accurately. Therefore, no guarantees are made.

If links are present, then it is possible that they may change or even not work for many reasons beyond the control of the author and/or distributors. Furthermore, the author cannot guarantee or otherwise be responsible for what you might find when you click through to sites not under the control of the publisher of this book.

It is the reader's sole responsibility to seek professional advice before taking any action on their part.

Preface

If you've used the Amazon search facility and found this book among their search results, well done! Trust me—and I am 100% sincere on this—there are, quite literally, hundreds of self-publishing books available and it's approaching the 'needle in a haystack' situation. But, it could be argued, this isn't such a bad thing.

Sure, there are a lot of titles to choose from—almost to the point where you could possibly be getting overwhelmed—but, with features such as *Look inside!* it gives you the opportunity to browse before you buy, and to see exactly what you're going to be getting.

Personally, I love looking at books in bookstores, reading a small part to better evaluate the material—exactly what you're doing here.

So, why do I think this book would be useful for you?

First, this book is aimed at beginners: whether it's with Microsoft Word or with self-publishing (to CreateSpace and/or the KDP).

If your Microsoft Word skills are a little more advanced, then that's okay too, as I've been Technical Writer and a Word power-user (some might say expert) for 17 and 20 years, respectively; and might be able to teach you a trick or 3; and, if you're better at the publishing element, then you're seriously going to have a blast!

Second, you see, as well as being a technical writer (and writer), I've also been teaching in one form or another since 1986; I've written numerous training guides, online help systems, developed my own apps, and other things around education and writing. Consequently, this skill-set enables me to bring something special to this process and helps ensure that I can make your entire book creation as easy and as seamless as possible.

Furthermore, and more importantly, I've written hundreds of reports, books, manuals, over the last 20-years; and, in the last 6 years of self-publishing, have published dozens of books on CreateSpace and Kindle (10 of my own/my wife's), and I use this exact same process every time: I know Word can be incredibly frustrating—often to the point of bewilderment—and this is how I know, with my help, this book will work for you.

As such, all you need to do is follow the step-by-step written and illustrated procedures in this book, and then you can do what I've done dozens of times—it really is straightforward.

Yes, Word can be a pain, but you can get one of my professional book templates for free from **http://www.1clickbookcreation.com/links/freetemplate.php** (it's free, no opt-in required); so, not only do I take all that hassle away, but you get a 6"x 8" *Kindle* template (that I use myself), to make the whole process even easier. Moreover, you may, understandably, want to change the look and feel for your book, so I also show you exactly how to modify that template yourself: that way, you know you are guaranteed to succeed and see your book on the virtual-shelf in record time.

Just a note on this template, it is the exact one I use for myself and my clients, and I am 100% confident it will work for you. As such—and this is my guarantee to you—if for whatever reason, within 6 months of you buying the book and following the steps given, you don't get your book self-published, then I want you to promise me that you'll email me and tell me that: then, not only will I refund your money, but I do my best to work with you to help you self-publish your book on CreateSpace and Kindle—that is my promise to you: my contact details are at the back of the book.

Finally, becoming a self-published author is a life-defining moment, even more so if you've done all the work yourself; and, if I've played some small part in this, whether with this book or the template, then feel free to drop me a line and let me know—I enjoy helping others, and I'd really appreciate it your news.

I wish you all the best with your writing, your formatting, and your publishing.

Russ Crowley

August 2017

Table of Contents

Abbreviations

Table of Figures

Table of Tables

1. Introduction

With the advent of the World-Wide Web and the advances in technology, it was only a matter of time before the publishing industry opened itself up to the general public. Yes, I do realize that it was kind of open to everyone before that, but realistically, for whatever reason, it was simply beyond the reach of many.

Now, with the number of self-publishing companies and the myriad of options available, every single person who has ever dreamed of seeing their words in a published format can do so; all it takes is a little effort and a little guidance. Indeed, even if you have no idea of how to put your words into print, there are people out there who do know how to do what you need; and, not only are they easy to find, but they are easy to contact and converse with.

Of course, external assistance outside of your immediate friends and family is unlikely to be free, but that doesn't mean that it has to be expensive. Sure, we have to be realistic about this (and you will need to calculate how much external assistance you need), and though there's a distinct correlation between costs and the level of service, you can offset some of this by using self-education-type websites where people are willing to pass on their knowledge for free; and you can start covering some of these deficiencies yourself (thereby reducing the assistance needed).

As an example, if you don't have Microsoft Word, Open Office is free, and so is their help. Also, I don't think I've ever seen a YouTube video you have to pay for, so if you haven't a clue about how to format your manuscript, go to YouTube and search for videos on how to do this. It's never been easier to learn to do more yourself.

Sure, if you have to pay someone to do the whole formatting, proofing, and editing, it's going to cost you; but, if you self-educate and learn to do what you can, and then get a friend or two to proof your manuscript, then you'll only need someone to edit your work— much less of a cost than paying for all three.

Your dream then becomes reality.

1.1.   Available Routes

Once your manuscript has been completed, you can pick the "route" you wish to take with your book. You can either opt for the "print route" (Print on Demand - POD), or the electronic route (eBooks); or, you can mostly opt for both. Naturally, there are a few differences between them, and I'll come to those in a moment, but first let's look at each individual route.

1.1.1. *Print-on-Demand*

The "print route" is where you submit your book to self-publishing companies such as CreateSpace, Lightning Source, Lulu, etc., and use these 'on-demand' services.

__Note__: I don't include Smashwords in this group as, though they provide a service to authors, it's a meat-grinder (their term, not mine); and, my one and only experience with them was a book I purchased to view on my iPhone in 2010. Had I been the author, I would not only have been appalled at the finished product but would have withdrawn my book immediately.

They may have improved since then, I don't know; but, as I say, though they do provide a service, it isn't for everyone.

> *Besides, one of the reasons for me writing this book is to equip you with the skills so you don't need to go within a hundred miles of them.*

In pre-self-publishing days, if you couldn't get a publisher for your book, but still wanted to see your book in print, you would have to pay a printer up-front for your book to be printed out. Bearing in mind the time, the effort, the materials, etc., to just do a single print run of your book would require you to purchase many hundreds of copies of your book for it to be cost-effective for the printers.

Afterwards, you yourself would probably have to arrange transport of your books to your place of storage, which for most, in all necessity, would be a room in the home or even the garage. Ultimately, it wasn't cheap and, again, probably beyond the financial or realistic reach of many.

Nowadays, there is no upfront cost for a print-run, you don't need to set aside storage space, and you don't have to worry about stacks of your books gathering unwanted dust. POD means that your book is only printed when an order is received. There is no wastage and there is no out-of-pocket expense.

What's more, not only do the self-publishing companies manage all this for you, they also advertise your book for you on their own and other websites; and, when they receive an order, they process it, ensure that the book is printed and bound, packaged, labelled, and shipped to your customer. Then, you'll either receive a check in the post, or a deposit in your bank account. How cool and simple is that?

In return for doing all of this, they take their cut out of your royalties; but, given the service they provide and the ease of the entire process, it's worth it (in my view). Besides, it's a business and with regards to CreateSpace (and my opinion), a very good one at that.

1.1.2. Electronic Books

For eBooks, from an author's book-creation process point-of-view, not much changes. Yes, you do have to do things slightly differently in terms of formatting and layout, but that's purely because e-format has different requirements than a printed copy; and, as each electronic device has slightly different requirements to the many others available, they all want their additional little tweaks: odt, doc, pdf, html, mobi, epub—apparently standardization is just short of four 4-letter words! But, in terms of your manuscript, nothing changes, you don't modify the words, it's just the layout, the pagination, and the formatting.

Over the last year or so, CreateSpace/Amazon (CreateSpace is an Amazon company) has tried to bridge the gap between the two routes by introducing functionality to seamlessly submit your print-copy manuscript to the Kindle Desktop Publishing (KDP) system (we'll just call it Kindle for ease of handling); but, this isn't the place to talk about that here.

Suffice it to say, at this stage I would advise against it, but will go into more detail why in section 4. For now though, we're going to look at publishing a printed version of your book with CreateSpace.

1.2.   Why CreateSpace?

When my partner, Duangta, and I were writing *Learning Thai, Your Great Adventure*—our first book to be self-published in 2010—I was looking at all the self-publishing options that were available.

To be honest, most of the companies were *much-of-a-muchness*, by which I mean they were all offering pretty much the same thing, at the same price, with one or two slight variations to make their packages slightly different from their competitors. Overall though, there wasn't much difference between them.

CreateSpace, however, was different.

You see, all the other companies sold you a design, formatting, and publishing package which meant that even if you had the ability to do some or all of the elements of the book creation process yourself, you still had to buy the package that closely resembled the services you needed. But ultimately, if you could do some of these yourself, there was no flexibility in the package, and you couldn't select or deselect individual components.

CreateSpace didn't have this inflexibility.

Sure, they had these services if you needed them, but if you didn't, it wasn't forced on you.

At the time, I had been a Technical Writer for around 13 or so years, and I was top-notch at most of the things needed: writing, setup, formatting, proof-reading, and so forth. In fact, the only thing I couldn't really do well—and still can't—was graphic design: I consider myself design-inept as, though I can modify designs pretty well, I struggle with the idea and what will look good; it's a weak area for me.

So, given the price and time aspect, why should I pay someone to do something which I can do myself? It made no sense then and it still makes no sense now; and is why, to this day, I still prefer CreateSpace over the other companies. Sure, today, one or two of the others probably allow you to do this, but they didn't then.

In addition, something I only found out after I'd published with them is that their help and support system is on-the-whole excellent too.

But, before we look at getting started with CreateSpace, why Microsoft Word?

1.3.   Why Word?

Well, apart from it being, arguably, the leading authoring package available, you know that Microsoft are going to be around for a long time to come.

Please don't send me emails telling me that I've got either of the above completely wrong, it's just my opinion, okay?

Feel free to disagree, but in the last 17-years as a Technical Writer, I've used Open Office, Scrivener, Notepad (and Notepad ++), InDesign, Framemaker, and quite a few others.

Yes, of course Word has its faults—it has a lot of them—but it's a fantastic package if you work with it the way it's meant to be used. Unfortunately, that's the problem many people have, they don't know how it's meant to be used. Over the years, I have met many people who use Word and, I can say in all honesty, if I take my shoes and socks off I can easily count the number of people who use Word to its potential.

For example, a lot (and I mean "a lot") of work I get given to proof-read and edit in Word shows that most use it as a glorified version of Notepad: they begin typing, change the size of the font and make it bold for a heading, and so on; and, believe me, if that's all you want to do, then Open Office will save you a lot of money!

You see, Word has got so much power under the hood and it's there to be used if you want to know how to use it. Admittedly, if you're writing a novel, then the chances are you'll never need 80-90% of the functionality Word offers and, if you don't have Word, then you may be better off getting something like Scrivener (I like Scrivener, I have Scrivener on my Mac); but, I won't be using it for this kind of book, that's not what it's really designed for. Besides; if you didn't have Word, or intend to use it, then the chances are you probably wouldn't even be reading this book in the first place.

I know Word, I like Word, Word likes me (I think); or so I tell myself, considering the number of hours we have spent working together over the years; and, yes, I seriously realize that I need to get out more!

2. Formatting for CreateSpace

In this section, we're going to look at how to format our book using Word 2007, 2010, 2013 and 2016. Now, though there are quite a few differences between the applications with regards to added functionality for using online materials and interactivity, in terms of the difference between the versions, as far as creating a book for CreateSpace or for Kindle is concerned, they're pretty minimal: in that respect, Word really hasn't changed that much since I started using it in 1994.

With regards to layout and design, as there is little difference, it shouldn't affect your ability to create a book on any of the platforms. This book was initially written using Word 2013. In early 2016, I upgraded to Word 2016 and, in terms of creating, formatting, and publishing books, the process is identical.

If you're still using Word 2007, the major difference is newer versions have a **design** menu, but the bulk of that's in the 2007 version's **Layout** menu .

In the following sections, we will look at setting up our Word environment so that it functions the way we want it to (and not the way Microsoft thinks it wants us to), how to setup your pages, use styles, section breaks, navigating within Word, and so on.

2.1. Setup Word

So, to get started and to work effectively, it's vital that you set Word up exactly as you want it. Of course, Microsoft has already configured it to function in a certain way, and though that may be what they feel is the best way to work with the program, it's unlikely to be true: if you're not sure of this, click on **File,** then on **New** and search for books in the list of templates—I think you'll be disappointed with the search results; and that's why we need to tweak our Word environment from the default out-of-the-box way Word is setup.

With that in mind, I have a way that I like to work and it's that method I'll present to you now (with the reasons why, if applicable); but, bear in mind it's just the way I like to do things and as long as you refer back to this page, you can go back and alter the settings as you see fit.

1. The first thing we need to do is turn off automatic formatting and correction – go to **File > Options > Proofing > Autocorrect Options and** click on the **Autocorrect options** button[1].

2. On the **Autocorrect** tab, turn off:

    o Capitalize first letter of sentences

    o Capitalize first letter of table cells.

3. On the **Autoformat As You Typ**e tab

    o I set and apply styles myself so I turn off everything under "**Apply as you type**," and "**Automatically as you type**": I want to do these things myself so that I know they're correct, I don't want Word to try and second-guess me and get it wrong.

4. On the **Autoformat** tab

    o Under "**Apply**," I turn off **Automatic Bulleted Lists and List Styles**.

    o Under **"Replace,"** I turn off **Internet and network paths with hyperlinks**. Adding hyperlinks as-and-when is easy in Word.

5. Come out of **Autocorrect** but stay in **Word Options**:

6. Go to **Save**

    – Locate **Embed fonts in the file** and select it.

---

[1] In Word 2007 this is **File > Word Options...**

7. Go to "**Advanced**"

   – Under "**Editing Options**," deselect **Keep Track of Formatting**. If you don't, this will screw your style-set up as Word will track any and every single modification to the existing styles (and that's not something we really want).

   – Change **"Default Paragraph Style"** to **Body** (it's there somewhere in the long drop-down list).

8. Under **Image Size and Quality**:

   – For CreateSpace books, you want to select "**Do Not Compress Images in file**." This will increase the file size of your document, but it will provide better image output.

   One note on this, if your file size does get too large, then look at your image type and size. If you want to create a Kindle book from your CreateSpace book, then your images need to be either gif or jpeg; if they're not, then you will need to convert them, but it's a good idea to create them at the correct size in your image editing program before inserting them into Word.

This is quite important. If you are used to saving your files as png, tif, or some other format that is not **gif** or **jpeg**, then you're going to have to go back and change them for Kindle.

Therefore, even if you're not thinking about publishing to Kindle at the moment, my advice would be to use the **gif** or **jpeg** format in case you later decide to do so. You'll save yourself a lot of time.

   If this still proves problematic, you can always **deselect** the "**Do Not Compress Images in file**" option.

   – Set default target output to **220 dpi**.

These are the main options for a CreateSpace book, and will give you better control over what you need.

2.2.   Book Setup

Now we'll look at setting up your book. Word is great for documents, reports, calendars, flyers, etc., but it doesn't offer a great deal of help when setting up a book.

The first thing that you need to do here is to decide on the size of your book—your *trim size*—as any subsequent changes you make will cause you additional formatting work.

Note: I will show you how to setup your book in Word, but when it comes to entering information into the document (sections 2.2.4 onwards), I will be referring **explicitly** to styles that I've created in a sample template available to download for **FREE** at

http://www.1clickbookcreation.com/links/freetemplate.php

Many of the styles within any document: Heading 1, 2, 3, 4, Body Text, etc. are built-in Word styles, and it's always a good idea to use what Word has (it likes it better that way); but the other styles are what I have been using for years: Numbers 1, 2, 3, 4; Bullet, 1, 2, 3, 4, etc. I don't like Word's bullets & numbering feature and mine works perfectly.

If you're unsure of what you are doing, I would recommend getting that template as that way your book is already setup for you, all the styles are configured, and all you need to then is modify the page size, margins, and perhaps tweak the layout. Even if you don't use it, you can still use it as a reference point.

2.2.1. Set Page Size

CreateSpace has a list of trim sizes (refer to Appendix A.1), so ensure you know the dimensions that you will use, then:

1. Click on **Page Layout** on the menu bar.

2. Click on the **Size** button.

3. At the bottom of the dropdown, click on **More Paper Sizes**:

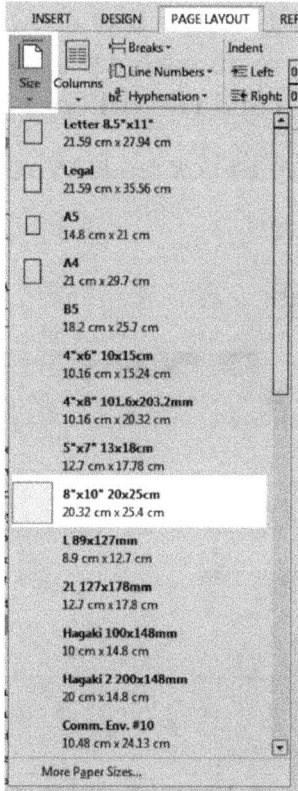

Figure 1 - More Paper Sizes

4. The following will display:

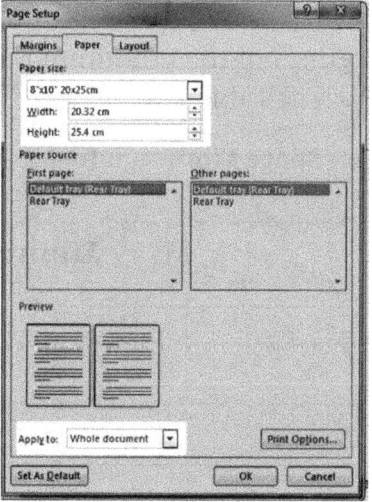

Figure 2 - Set Page Size

5. Don't worry about what the **preview** shows, or the **paper source**, just select the **page size** you require from the drop-down list, or enter the exact dimensions in the **Width** and **Height** boxes.

6. Make sure that the **Apply to** box reads **Whole document**.

2.2.2. *Set Margins*

7. Click on the **Margins** tab:

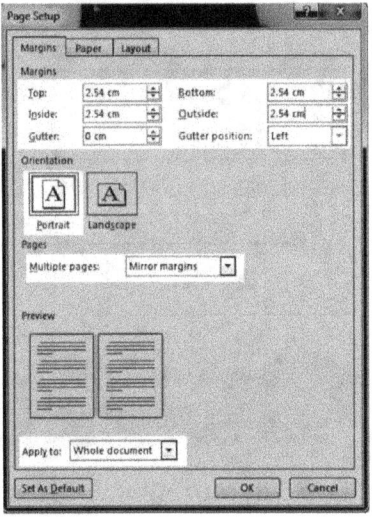

Figure 3 - Set Margins

8. Set your margins. CreateSpace requires a minimum of 0.5" on the **outside, top,** and **bottom** margins, but the minimum **inside** margin will depend on the page count, as shown in Table 1:

Table 1 – CreateSpace Minimum Inside Margin Sizes

Page Count	Minimum Inside Margin
24–150	0.375"
151–400	0.75"
401–600	0.875"
>600	1.0"

Note: if you do decide on one of the larger page sizes, then small margins looks unprofessional. Try it out and you'll see what I mean.

9. Make sure that **Mirror Margins** is selected: the preview will then display correctly and as show in Figure 2 and Figure 3.

2.2.3. Set Layout

10.   Click on the **Layout** tab:

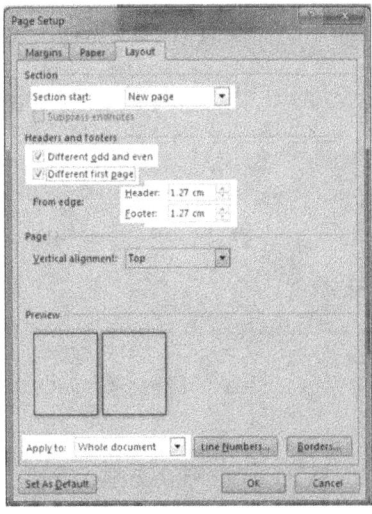

Figure 4 - Set Layout

11.   **Section Start** needs to be **New Page[2]**.

12.   **Headers & Footers** needs to be **Different odd and even**.

You can set your **Header & Footer** settings as you want, depending on your trim size (the size of the page: you might want to reduce these settings for smaller page sizes).

13.   If you want the first page of each new section to be different from the remainder of the section (as in this book), select **Different first page**.

14.   **Vertical alignment** is **Top**.

---

[2] In the earlier version of the book, I specified this as **Odd page**. However, since fault-finding manuscripts and publishing additional books, selecting **New page** as the section start is by far the easier and more manageable option.

15. **Apply to** needs to be **Whole Document**.

16. That's it, click on **Ok** to apply the page settings.

Please **Save** your document now.

2.2.4.Setup Your Title Page

One of the most important things that you can do when setting up your book from a blank page is to turn on **Show/Hide** characters. This shows exactly what you have on the page and where everything is. We'll do that now.

17. Go to the **Home** menu and click on the **Show/Hide characters** button:

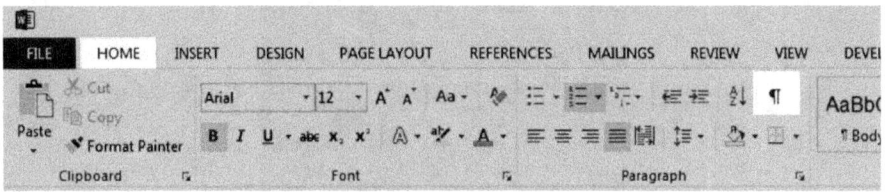

Figure 5 - Show/Hide Characters

Now we can see what we're doing.

18. With your cursor on the first line, in the **Styles** area of the ribbon, find **Title** and click on it (as shown in Figure 6).

19. Then, start typing your title in the document:

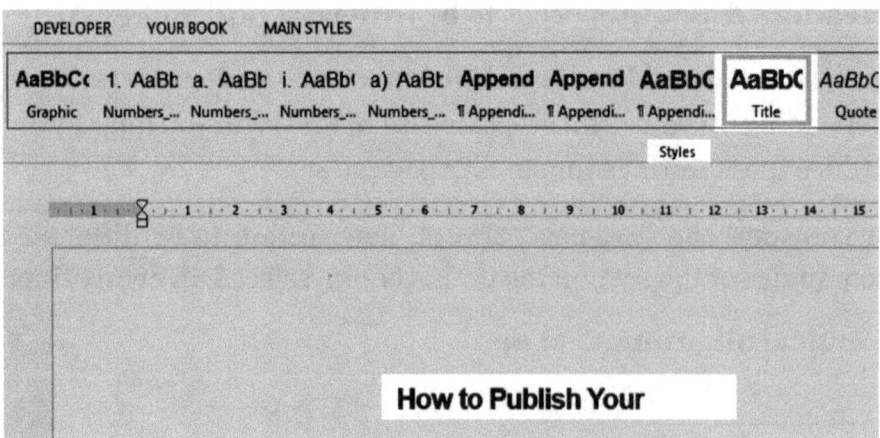

Figure 6 - Title Style and Entering Title

20. Press enter, and then enter your **subtitle**.

21. So on and so forth to enter your **author name** and **publisher name**.

22. After publisher, click on **Insert > Page break** to create a new page.

We can now setup the **Copyright page**.

2.2.5. *Setup Your Copyright Page*

One common structure of this page is to have the title at the top, followed by your web address, then your copyright information, ISBN number, disclaimer, and so on.

Please refer to the copyright page of this, or any other book to get ideas of how your own book should look (as shown in Figure 7):

Figure 7 - Image of This Book's Copyright Page

2.2.6. *Testimonials and Dedications*

The testimonials and dedications pages can be setup using a page break after your disclaimer and formatting the respective pages as required. Again, I encourage you to download the pre-configured template from **http://www.1clickbookcreation.com/links/freetemplate.php**

2.2.7. *Insert Table of Contents*

Your Table of Contents (ToC) should be on a new page, with the title at the top.

Click on **References** > **Table of Contents**, and select the type of ToC required:

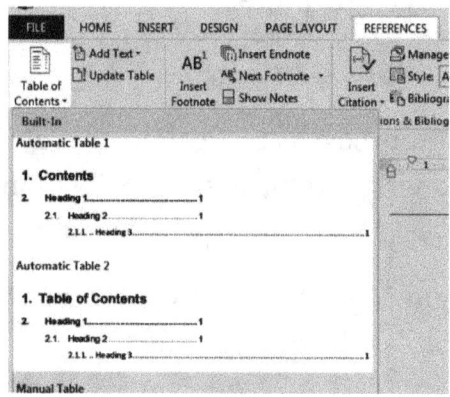

Figure 8 - Insert Table of Contents

This will insert the ToC at your cursor point.

2.2.8. *Headers & Footers*

Before you start modifying the header & footers (H&F) of your document, you need to understand about how Word works. When we initially created our book at the start of this section, we kept selecting **Whole Document** for "**Apply to**". There are other options in this setting, including **This Section**, and **This Point Forward**.

Word uses *sections* to partition or separate parts of the document or book; and, when you first set a document up, there is only one section. So any formatting or layout you apply to that document, particularly in the headers and footers, will replicate through that section.

With regards to H&F's, these are almost a "document behind a document" in Word, and as they are section-specific, act differently than the main document. As such, if you subsequently want to change the formatting of a section, to perhaps change the page numbering format or insert a landscape page, then you need to add a new section; or, more accurately, you need to add a new section and then tell Word that you want to do something different with that new section.

If you look at the first part of this book (the one you're now holding in your hands), the title page, copyright page, etc., you'll see that the pages don't have page numbers—this is one section (section 1); then, if you look at the ToC and the index pages, you'll see that it has lowercase Roman numerals as page numbers—this requires another section to distinguish it from the first (section 2); and, finally, if you look at the page number on these two pages, you'll see they are Arabic numbers—impossible without yet another section break (section 3). This is how Word works and uses sections (refer to section 2.4 for more details).

To enter the H&F area of your document, double-click on your document in the H&F area. You can now modify them accordingly. Alternatively, click on **Insert** on the menu bar, then you can see the options available:

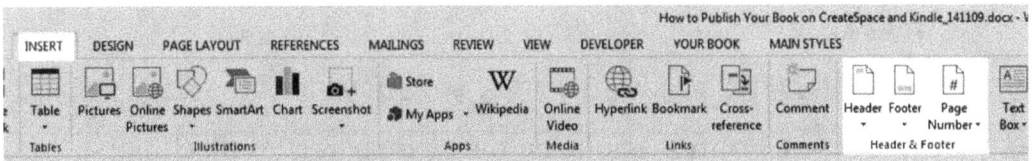

Figure 9 - Header & Footer Options

There are many options here. I would 1) recommend you download the template for ease of use and understanding; and/or, 2) explore the possibilities of using Word's built-in options.

2.2.8.1. *Entering the Header & Footer Areas*

There are two ways you can enter the H&F area, one has been described above, and the other is to:

- Click on **Insert** > **Header** > **Edit Header** (or **footer**).

Once you have done this, the H&F options will be available:

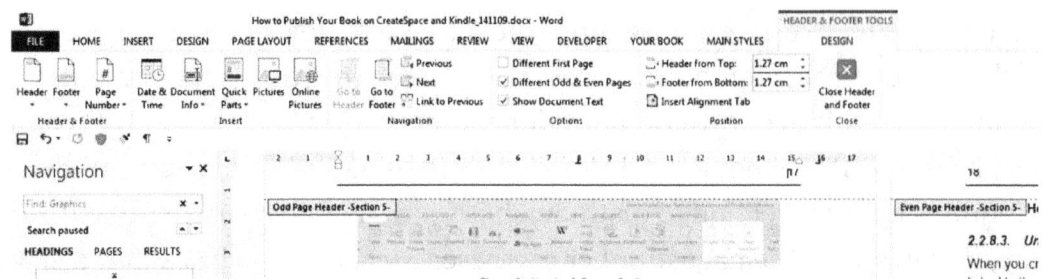

Figure 10 - Header & Footer Options

When you are in the H&F area, you can only function in these two areas. As mentioned, they are like a "document within a document".

2.2.8.2. *Exiting the Header and Footer Area*

There are two ways to exit the H&F area:

- Double-click on the body area of the page outside of the H&F.

- In **Header & Footer Tools**, on the menu bar, click on **Close**.

2.2.8.3. *Unlinking Sections*

When you create a new section, unless it is inserting columns, it is automatically linked to the one before it; and you can only do something different if you **unlink it**. Naturally, only linked sections can be unlinked (and vice-versa).

With your cursor in the H&F, you can easily see if they are linked as they will show a **Same as Previous** tag in the document, and the **Link to Previous** button will be highlighted (as shown in Figure 11):

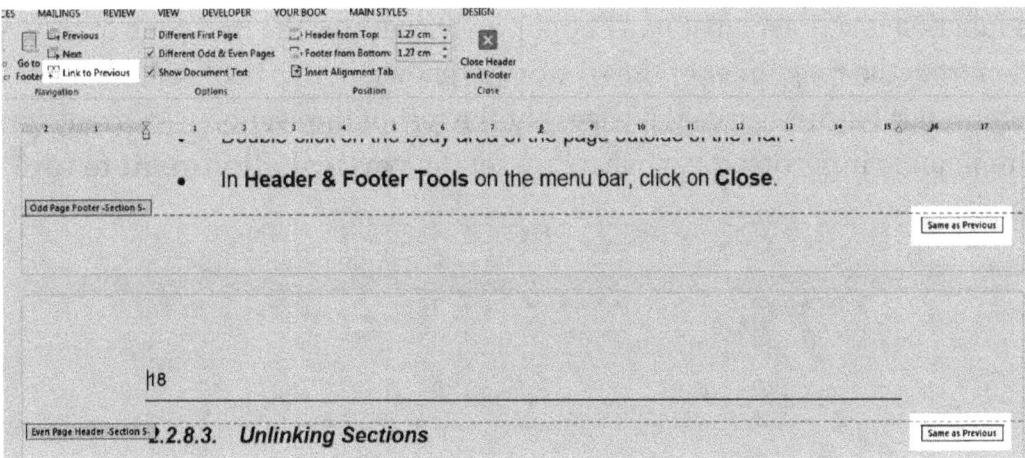

Figure 11 - Linked Header

To unlink the header (or footer), click on the **Link to Previous** button in the ribbon. The link will be broken. You can now modify that header or that footer, and it will not affect the previous one.

2.2.8.4. *Relinking Sections*

As you author your book and add or remove sections, you may find you need to relink sections, this is just a reverse of the above:

1. Open the H&F area (section 2.2.8.1).

2. Place your cursor in the required header or footer.

3. Click on **Link to Previous** (section 2.2.8.3), and the sections will relink.

Note: this usually messes up the contents of your header or footer, so my advice is to copy the contents of the header or footer that you will want to use after relinking, while simultaneously getting ready to use the **Undo** button (H&F's can be quirky).

2.2.8.5. *Different First Page*

Word offers an additional section/H&F function which is very useful called the **Different First Page** option.

This function is self-explanatory (I hope), and separates the first page of the new section from the remainder of the section (as shown in this book, where new chapters start halfway down the page, but the rest of the section is 'normal' (do you remember in section 2.2.3, where we set the **vertical alignment** to **top**?):

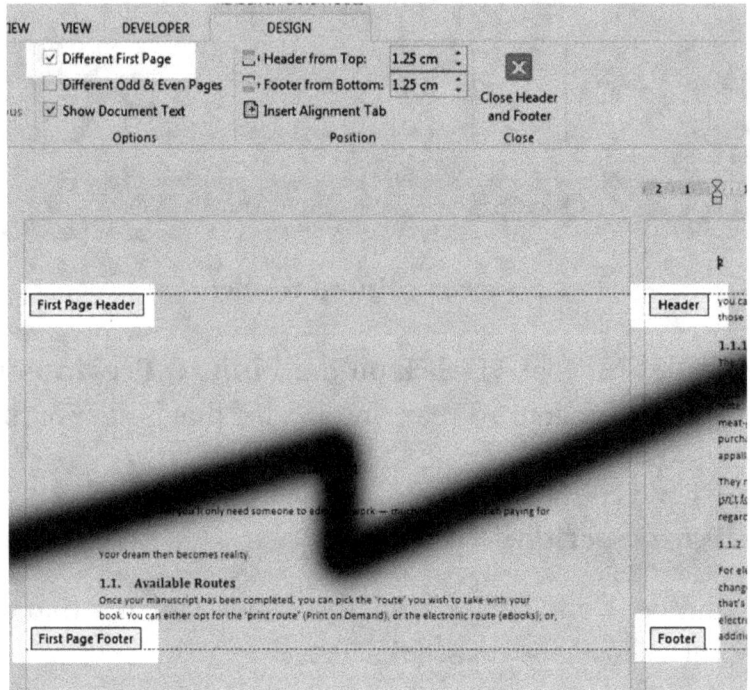

Figure 12 - Different First Page

To create a different first page:

1. Go into the header or the footer of the section that you wish to modify.

2. Click on **Different First Page.**

The first page H&F will be marked accordingly, and you can modify this as required.

Note: when writing your book, don't be tempted to insert a cover on (or as) the front page as CreateSpace and KDP both require separate interior and cover files to be submitted.

2.2.9. Page Numbering

As shown in section 2.2.8, you can insert page numbers from the **Insert > Headers & Footers** section.

2.2.10.   Adding Indexes

There are two methods of adding indexes, one is with the 1-Click Book Creation (1CBC) Template, as mentioned earlier, and the other is as detailed in section 2.2.10.2.

2.2.10.1. Adding an Index with 1CBC

With the template, three indexes are already in the template (four if you include the ToC), but if you've removed them and later want to replace them:

1. Place your cursor where you want to insert the index.

2. Click on **Insert** on the menu bar.

3. Click on **Quick Parts**.

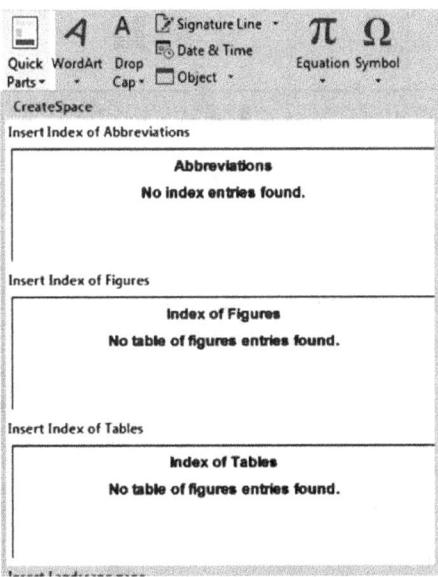

Figure 13 - Insert Index

4. Click on the type of Index that you require, and it will be inserted at your cursor point.

2.2.10.2. Adding Indexes Manually

Though you can add an unlimited number of indexes to your book, this section will cover adding an **Index of abbreviations**, an **Index of figures**, and an **Index of tables**.

2.2.10.3. Index of Abbreviations

To add an **Index of Abbreviations**:

1. Place your cursor where you want the index to go.

2. Click on **References** on the menu bar.

3. Click on **Insert Index**.

4. Select the type of index that you want, the format required, the number of columns, the tab leader, the language required, and any other requirements.

2.2.10.4. Index of Figures

To add an **Index of figures**:

1. Place your cursor where you want the index to go.

2. Click on **References** on the menu bar.

3. Click on **Insert Table of Figures**.

4. Select the type of index you want, the format required, the caption label, the page-number alignment, etc.

5. Click **Ok**. Your index will be inserted at your cursor.

2.2.10.5. Index of Tables

To add an **Index of tables**:

1. Place your cursor where you want the index to go.

2. Click on **References** on the menu bar.

3. Click on **Insert Table of Figures**.

4. Select **table** from the **caption label**.

5. Select the format required, whether page numbers are required, their alignment, etc.

6. Click **Ok**. Your index will be inserted at your cursor.

2.2.11. *Your Book's First Page*

The first page of the main body of your book should always start at **page 1** (or just 1), and be on a right-hand page. Throughout your book, this means odd-numbered pages are on the right-hand page, and even-numbered pages are on the left-hand page (the reverse or back of the page)—this is standard in publishing: pick up any book in your house and have a look at the front matter and initial layout.

To ensure that this happens:

1. If your first page will fall on a left/even-side page, then you need to insert an **odd-page** section break to insert a blank page, and **force** it onto the correct page—this also doesn't confuse Word when you try to specify an odd page number on an "even page" (remember back to section 2.2.3 and Figure 4, where we set different odd and even pages?)

2. If your first page does naturally fall on an odd-numbered/right-side page, then insert an odd-page break before it anyway to make sure (you will probably be changing the page numbering from Roman to Arabic numerals anyway, so you will need a section break).

   This will help us with laying out our book correctly with Word and is essential when setting up and working with your layout.

Once your front matter and first page are setup correctly, you can start typing your book and the pages will flow odd-even correctly. If you have your odd and even page numbers on the outside of your margins, and your even page numbers are on the same side of the page as your odd pages, double-click on the header and then left-align the even numbered page.

Figure 14 shows what you want to achieve, as well as two possible incorrect outcomes.

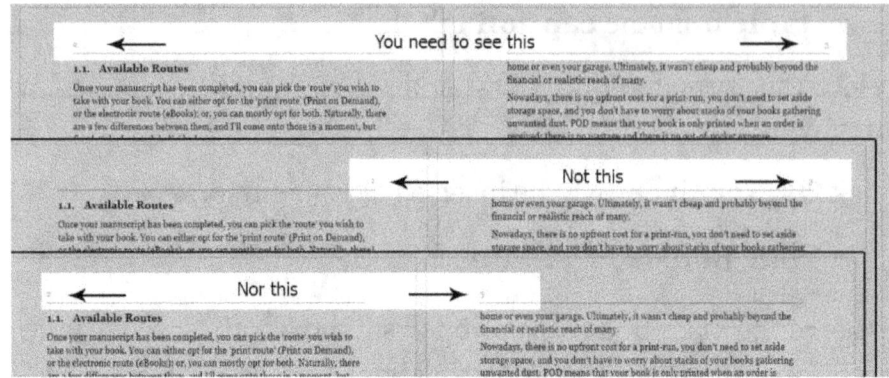

Figure 14 - Correct Page Number Positioning

Some may say that page numbers should be centered in the footer, but you can do what you're happy with. I usually go for header, outside-aligned (as in this book).

2.3. Using Styles

Right, now it's time to get into the nitty-gritty, but first, a question for you...

> *Do you know what the biggest cause of failure or frustration for people using Word, or giving up on Word, is?*

Styles!

Yes styles are the one single reoccurring, over-riding, major factor which contributes to people's inability to use Word correctly, and which leads to frustration, to lost work, corrupt documents, errors, and general nightmares!

I'll say it again – it's styles.

And, for the third time – it's **styles**!!!!

Conversely, if you do learn how to use them—they really aren't that difficult, I think, it's more about awareness—then 90% of your problems with Word will vanish, instantly.

In over 17 years of working with documents and templates in a professional capacity, I have found that this is the **single biggest cause of failure** or complaints.

Luckily for you, that is all about to change.

First, they're simple to implement correctly and all the styles you will probably ever need, or at least the vast majority of them, are already in the sample template.

I have to admit, at one point, I was considering locking the template down so you couldn't create or enter any more styles, but that wouldn't be fair to you because, at this initial stage, getting to grips with Word is part of the learning curve, and when you understand what's occurring, when things do eventually go wrong—and they will, I guarantee it—you will better understand why.

Then, not only does your skill improve, but you also become far more efficient at what you're doing; and, though I know you're punishing yourself by going through this book, surely that's the whole point of this exercise?

So without further ado, what do we actually mean when we are talking about styles?

Well, Word uses three main types of styles:

- Paragraph styles
- Character styles
- Section styles.

Note: it could be argued that now Word also incorporates table styles, list styles, and all that, but that is over-complicating matters at this early stage.

For the small list above, though the last item is handy to know—and is essential to know if you want to go on to build your own solid, professional templates—they are actually in order of importance, so we'll look at them in that sequence.

2.3.1. Paragraph Styles

When you open a new document in Word and that blank, bright, white page stares out at you, you have 3 options: 1) run and hide (or the equivalent), 2) stare right back, or 3) start typing.

If you suffer from panic, need a coffee, would rather do this another day, or something similar, then it'll probably be 1; if you suffer from writer's block, it'll be 2; if you're fearless, have no idea what I'm talking about, or have either conquered or don't suffer from writer's block then it'll be 3; and, if it is, you begin typing.

Now, you may or may not know this, but straight away, before you've even hit that first key, before that initial character graces that canvas and becomes the foundation of that power word, that thought-provoking sentence, and that insightful paragraph, Word has already decided what it thinks you want.

Word is in control.

Of you and your book.

But, we don't want that. We want control; and, we need to take it back.

As you may or may not already know, Word will eventually screw you up if you don't. It always does.

So let's take this control back...

If you click on the **Home** tab and look on the ribbon at the styles section in the right-middle part of the toolbar, you'll see that one of the styles is highlighted (as shown in Figure 15):

Figure 15 - Body Style on the Ribbon

The main/text style we use in this template is called **Body** (it's short for body text). Body text is the text you use to type into the main **body** of your document. As this style sits on the ribbon in the **Styles** section and, when you apply this style, it affects the entire paragraph. As it effects the entire paragraph, it's called (strangely enough) a **paragraph style**.

This is kind of easy and little can go wrong in that first paragraph. The problems creep in with subsequent paragraphs.

You see, and I have seen this **thousands of times**, the most common problem with people working with styles is that when they've finished typing the sentence, or writing their heading, they press the return key.

Then, they start typing a new sentence, which could be a new heading, it could be a list item, or it could be something else entirely.

This then continues throughout their document.

At some point, the author then goes back to a point in their document, they highlight the text, then they do something with it to make it stand out: make it larger, underline it, change the color, whatever it is they require; and, then they carry on to the next place and the next and do similar. And again. And again.

The problem is, though the underlying paragraph style is still the same, every modification to every character, word, sentence, or even paragraph, has to be remembered by Word.

As you can quite possibly imagine, this uses up far more memory than it should; and, when you also factor in the number of pages in a long document, lots of images, tables, and everything else, it all adds to the document size and time to load. When you subsequently reopen the document, Word has to remember every single modification you've made before it can display it; and, from Word's perspective, <u>what a pain!</u>

This is, without a shadow of a doubt, ***THE*** biggest cause of corrupted documents and crashes in Word, especially in older, slower machines—Word just couldn't handle it.

> *In 2012, a client asked me to sort their dissertation out as it kept crashing and they couldn't work on it.*
>
> *It was over 200-pages, 20 MB in size, and contained about 25 images and a number of tables.*
>
> *On inspection, the entire APA-style document: headings, body text, references, quotations, footnotes, [manual] Table of Contents, Figures, and Tables, everything... was all in "Normal" style.*
>
> *It took me about three hours to format their document and, on completion, the file size was under 2MB in size and it no longer crashed.*
>
> *The solution?*
>
> *Styles.*

So, for *each different element* of your document, use a different style. For example, this is the **Body** style and every [body] paragraph that requires this style, uses it. I don't have any other style to perform this function:

1-style = 1-function

Naturally, other document elements require different styles:

Section 3   This is the Heading 1 style for this document

3.1.   This is the Heading 2 Style

This is Body Text and below this paragraph are a selection of the main styles I setup in my document (**http://www.1clickbookcreation.com/links/freetemplate.php**).

This is the **ParaIndent** style which, if I indented the first-line of my body text (above), I would ensure that it was aligned here; but, in this document, my body text is left-aligned.

2.1.2.   *This is the Heading 3 style.*

- This is the **Bullet_L1** style (level 1).

  This is the **Indent 1** style (it aligns with Bullets and Numbers Level 1). It has a deeper indent than **ParaIndent** (plus it keeps the 1's, the 2's, etc., together).

  - This is Bullet_L2

    This is Indent 2

    o This is Bullet_L3.

       This is **Indent 3.**

       a) This is Numbers_L4.

       ⇒ This is Bullet_L4.

          This is **Indent 4**. There isn't an Indent 5 as we're running out of horizontal space on the page as we go across.

1. This is Number_L1.

   This is the **Indent 1** again.

   So is this.

   b. This is Numbers_L2.

      This is **Indent 2** again.

      i. This is Numbers_L3.

      This is **Indent 3.**

So you can see, the styles are defined and designed to allow your document to both flow and align correctly: both are essential components of an easy to read, professional-looking document.

The key point here is that these styles are defined to do...

...**1 job** and only **1 job**!

They don't do anything else.

The previous stand-out text style is called the **Important** style, and I use it to make the text stand-out and to bring attention to what I'm saying. In black & white text (in the print copy book), it won't be particularly clear or visible, but you can see that the border draws attention to the text and the message therein.

In the same way that you wouldn't use a hammer as a screwdriver—trust me, neither the tool nor the nail will thank you for it—don't use the Body style where you need a heading and don't use the Body style to create a list—<u>Word doesn't like it</u> and **it will mess you up**.

If not today, then maybe tomorrow; most certainly at some point.

However, we do have a bit of flexibility with paragraph styles in that we can modify individual elements of them if we want; and this is where **character styles** come in.

2.3.2. Character Styles

As the name confusingly suggests, character styles can be applied to individual characters in your document. However, if you wanted to, you could also apply character styles to words, sentences, paragraphs, sections; in fact, the whole document if you want. There's nothing stopping you, but again it's not what they're designed for, so Word will most likely slap you down at some point.

Like the other types of style, **they're there for a purpose**, they allow you to apply specific formatting to your text *without affecting the overall paragraph style*; and, are used mostly to provide some form of emphasis.

If you see what I've done in the preceding paragraph, I've added a bold style font to the first clause, and italicized part of the second—I'm emphasizing these so they stand out.

Of course, if I used a paragraph style to do this, then all the text in the paragraph would be affected, but by using character styles only the attributes of the selection are modified, such as: **Si*ze***, color, highlighting, ~~strikethrough~~, superscript, subscript, borders , underline, double underline, s p a c i n g   AND   positioning, etc., while leaving the remainder of the paragraph alone. **Note**: YOU CAN EVEN CHANGE THE FONT TYPE AND IT WILL NOT AFFECT THE PARAGRAPH STYLE; however, the underlying paragraph style is still **Body**.

As such, they have one purpose and, once again, aren't used for anything other than what they're designed for.

2.3.2.1. *Removing Character Styles*

To remove character styles:

1. Select the text containing the character styles you want to remove.

2. Click on **Clear All Formatting** on the font ribbon:

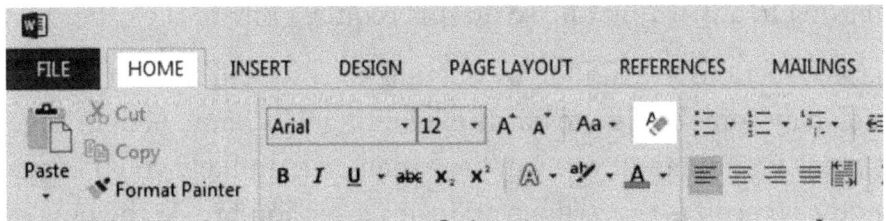

Figure 16 - Clear All Formatting

That will clear the formatting from your selection.

We'll now look at the third type of style in Word, section styles.

2.3.3. *Section Styles*

Sections refers to individual parts (or sections) of your document and the specific formatting that part contains. When you start a new document, you usually have a single page–that is your first section and you can do what you wish here: you can resize the page, the page margins, add a header, a footer, page numbers, etc.

Anything you do will just affect this single section (you only have the one, so it can't affect anything else).

If you then decide you want to do something different to the layout of the next page, such as insert a landscape-oriented page between two portrait-oriented pages, then you cannot do this with a page break, you need a section break.

Similarly, if you have a single column of text on a page, but then decide you want to change the on-page layout to multiple columns, you need a section break.

Though there are multiple sub-types of break: continuous, next page, odd, even, etc., these can be grouped into 3 main types:

- page break
- column break
- section break.

First, **and this is extremely important**, a page break is **not** a section break, it performs an entirely different function. A page break will insert a new page and place your cursor at the top of that new page, but you cannot then change the page formatting in any way at all. To do this requires one of the other two breaks.

Unfortunately, sections are hidden by default, so you need to turn them on to see them (which may somehow go towards explaining why some people have so many problems with them: if you can't see them, it's unlikely you'll know they're there). Another reason is that when you insert a section break, the new section is usually "connected" to the previous section which, when you consider that the main reason for adding a new section on a different page is probably because you want to change the page formatting, is bordering on illogical (though there are other reasons you can add them, but this is by far the most common).

2.3.4. Modifying Styles

Creating or modifying styles is easy, but bear in mind that the more styles you have, the easier it is to either lose control, or for your book to look poor.

Again, if you want to trust my experience and use the styles that I use, get the template. Sure, I fully expect you to want to change the look and feel, but you can do that by copying the template, leaving the original as-is, and then modify the styles in the copy. That way, there's little danger of messing anything up.

There are a number of ways to modify the styles, but if all you wish to do is change the overall font, this takes seconds...

2.3.4.1. *Change the Base Font*

Some Word users will often use the built-in 'Normal' style as what is often termed 'the base font', as well as using it as the *Default Paragraph Style*); but, in this template, I use the **Body** style as the main body font (remember when we selected it back in section 2.1, number 7, bullet 2?).

This then allows us to redefine or customize the **Body** font as we require, and the **Normal** style remains untouched. Then, by basing the other styles on the **Normal** style, we can modify them individually without risking accidentally modifying any others.

If we subsequently want to change something throughout the document then we just change the **Normal** style, and everything replicates through. Believe me, it might not sound like much, but it does make a huge difference, as well as making the template more manageable and stable.

To change the base font (the base font is the main font in the book):

1. Locate the **Normal** style on the style ribbon:

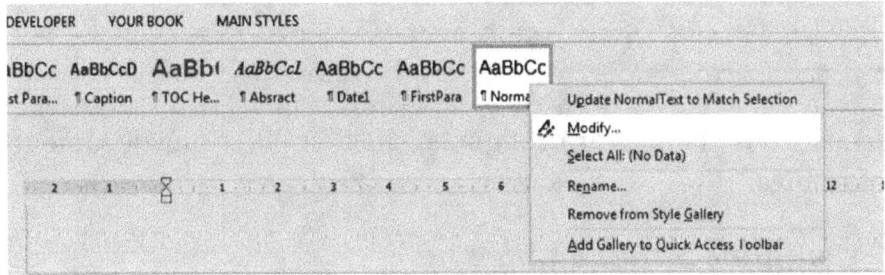

Figure 17 - Change Base Font

2. Right-click on it and select **Modify** (as shown in Figure 17).

3. Select the new font that you wish to use:

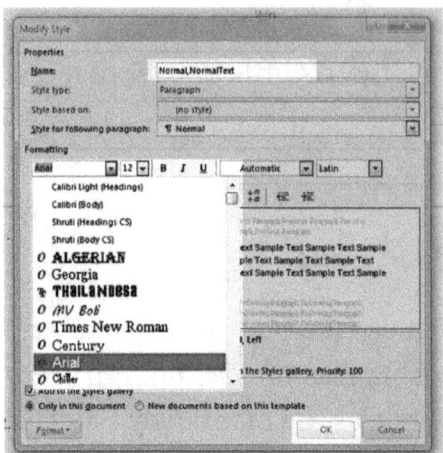

Figure 18 - Select New Base Font

4. You can modify the other font features in this template here, such as size, color, etc., but bear in mind that most, if not all, of the other styles are **based** on this **Normal** style, so if you change these attributes here, you could inadvertently affect all the other styles.

> My advice is to just change the font name or, if your book has large print, perhaps you can increase the font size; but, other than that, be prepared for weird things to happen. Some fonts have different spacing, so what might look good in *Times New Roman*, won't necessarily look good in *MV Boli*, or *Bookman Old Style.*

Note: after making any changes to the 'Normal' style\base font, always check how your other styles look.

---

5. Once all your changes are complete, click on **Ok**. Your document font will now change.

2.3.4.2. *Modifying Styles on the Fly*

The easiest way to modify an existing style is to insert a blank line, type in some text, format that line/text exactly how you want your style to look and then tell Word to use that new definition:

1. Insert a blank line (press return or enter on your keyboard).

2. Type in "Sample text."

3. Format that piece of text **exactly** how you want that style to look.

    For example, I want to change my **Important** style to Algerian font with a double-wavy lined border (why, I don't know, but this illustrates my point); so, I type my text and I format the sample text **exactly** how I want it (size, color, borders, paragraph indents, etc.):

    ╔══╗
    ║   SAMPLE TEXT   ║
    ╚══╝

4. Then, I go to the **styles ribbon**, find the style that I want to modify (as shown in Figure 19):

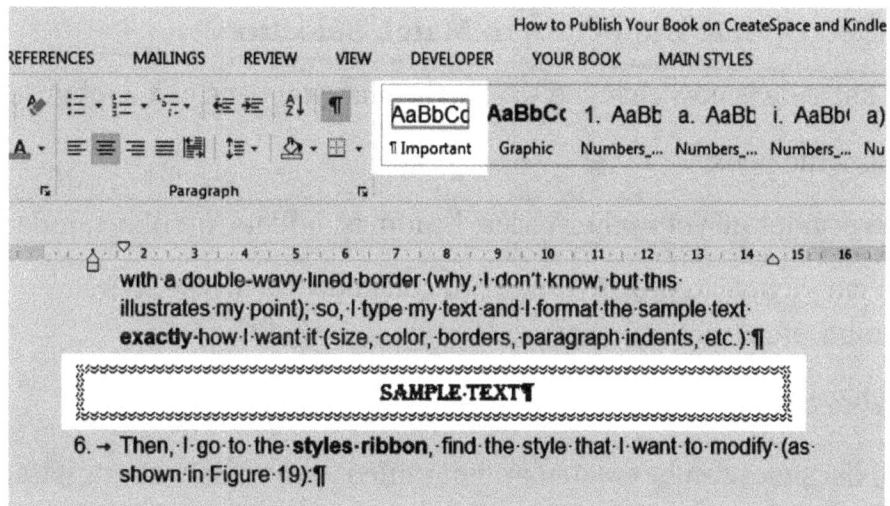

Figure 19 - Identify the Style

5. Right-click on the **style:**

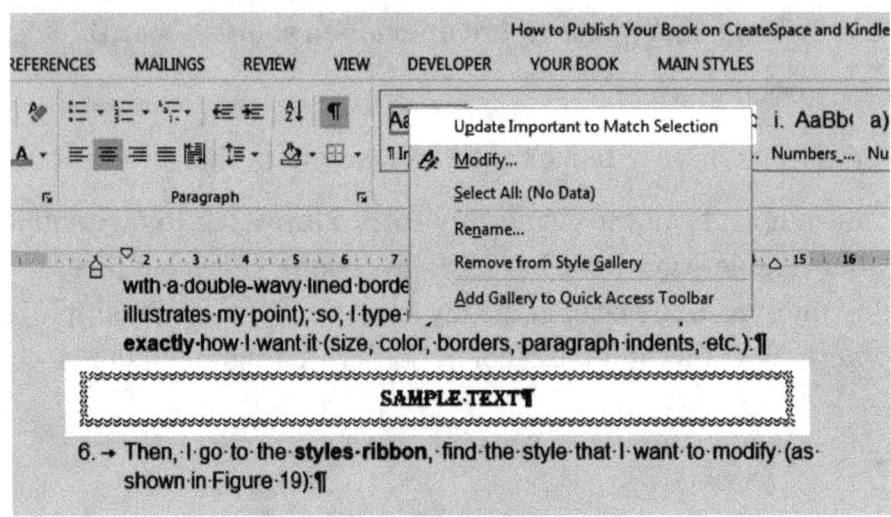

Figure 20 - Update Existing Style

6.   Select **Update Important to Match Selection**.

That style is now changed to exactly what you have just configured.

7.   Save the book.

8.   Repeat for all your other styles: headings, bullets, numbers, indents, etc.

Now, you have a book template unique to you and with all the styles, configuration, etc., from my original. How good is that?

2.3.5. *Table Styles*

Table and list styles can be created and modified in the same way as paragraph and character styles and, as such, is not something that I particularly worry about. Yes, I do use table styles, but I prefer to select and use an existing style than to create my own, mainly because there are a ton of table styles available and it is so easy.

To insert a table and modify it:

1.   Click on **Insert** on the menu bar.

2.   Click on the arrow at the bottom of the **Table** button and insert the required table dimensions (column and rows).

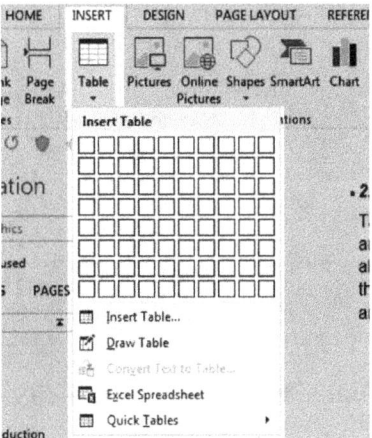

Figure 21 - Insert Table

You can do this by selecting from the grid, or you can click on **Insert Table** and follow the dialog.

Once your table is in your book:

3. Place your cursor somewhere in the table, and **Table Tools** will appear on the menu bar

4. Click on the **Design** menu, and you can see the **Table Styles:**

Figure 22 - Table Styles

5. Select the table style that you require from the available styles, and your table will change to that style.

6. Right-click on the table style in the ribbon, and select **Modify Table Style:**

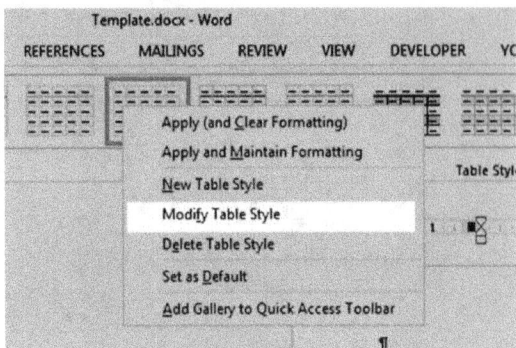

Figure 23 - Modify Table Style

7. You will then be able to modify the various elements of the table:

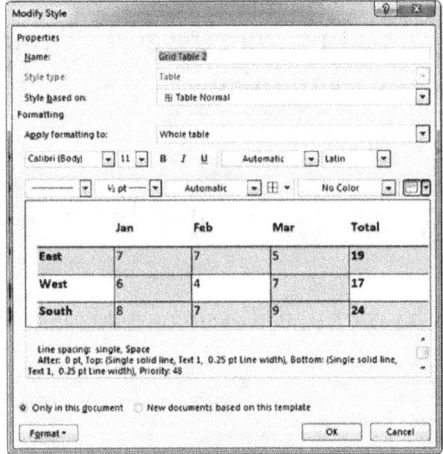

Figure 24 - Modifying the Table Style

8. Don't expect to get it right your very first time, but play about with the settings so that it reflects exactly what you want. Then, once you're done, click on **OK** to save the changes.

9. If you wish to use this as your default table style (and for consistency in your book, I would thoroughly recommend that you do), right-click on the table style in the ribbon and select **Set as Default**.

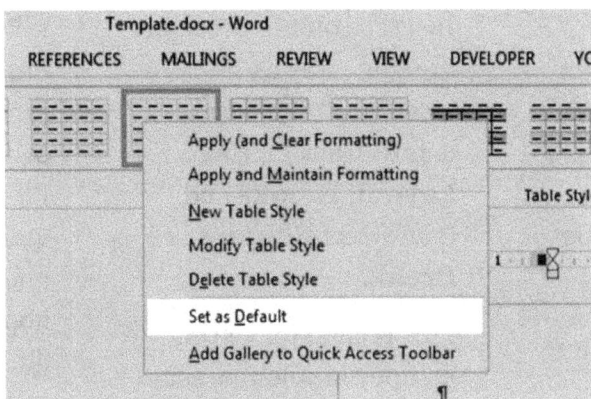

Figure 25 - Set as Default

Note: remember that Kindle does not accept tables. You will need to take an image of each table in your book and reinsert it as an image in your Kindle version.

2.4.   Section Breaks

As mentioned briefly in 2.3.3, sections refers to the different parts of your document, and adding section breaks permits you to modify the look-and-feel of your book, as well as to alter the pagination of the next section, such as: change portrait to landscape, change the page size (if you so wish), the page color, etc.

Again, though there are a few different kinds of section break, they can be categorised as *next page* and *on-page*. Next page breaks allow you to modify the subsequent section which will begin on the following page; in contrast, one of the principal functions of the on-page break—called a **continuous break**—is to allow you to change the column layout on that and subsequent pages [but it doesn't force an initial page break].

To illustrate this, I've added some multi-column text in the following section. This is easy to do. Click on **Page Layout > Columns > [one/two/three, etc.]** and Word will insert the required number of columns for you.

2.4.1. Column Breaks

For example, this paragraph and the heading above are a single-column block of text. If you want to insert columns, then you need to select the text of your document... (please continue reading the column text, left-to-right):

... (with your mouse normally), then click on **Page Layout**, and then click on **Columns** before selecting the number of columns you require.

Insert a column break in the same way as I inserted a page break before. Click on **Page Layout**, **Breaks** and then select **Column Break**.

This is good for setting up uneven columns such as I have in this particular

selection, and would be impossible without the functionality that the column break affords. I'll be honest, it's unlikely I would use uneven columns, but hopefully it helps illustrate what I'm trying to explain.

As my point is now complete, the next paragraph will be single-column text again.

I appreciate that this may be kind of confusing at the moment, but press **Ctrl+Shift+8** on your keyboard, it will show the following:

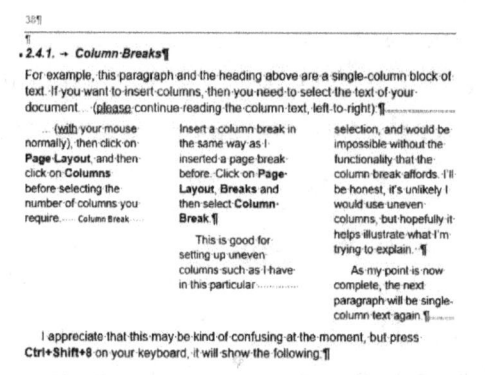

Figure 26 - Column Breaks

Hopefully, you can see the different breaks we've applied in Figure 26 (there are four of them), but in case you can't, I've highlighted them in Figure 27:

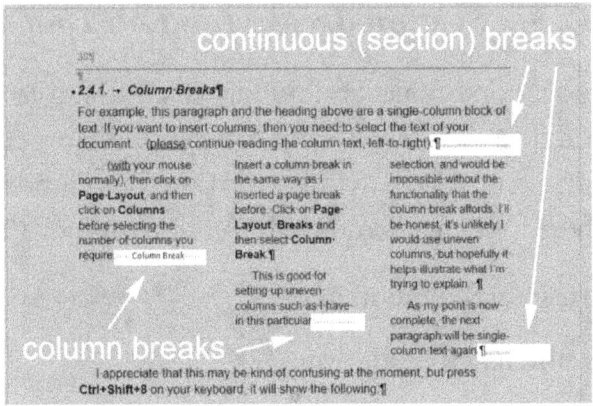

Figure 27 - Highlighted Column Breaks

Figure 27 shows the **section breaks** that Word inserts to differentiate this section (the top and bottom shaded breaks) and the 2 in-**column breaks**; and, by moving the text between these breaks around, I can control the exact flow of my columns.

Note that the top and bottom breaks—**continuous breaks**, as opposed to **column breaks**—allows us to change the formatting on the same page, thereby **continuing** the document flow. It's the column breaks themselves which do the separating of columns.

In other words, the section breaks "break" the formatting flow of the column-section from both the single-column text before and after it—picture an island with water flowing around it. Please note, if you accidentally delete any of these section breaks, then weird things will happen (it's this whole **unlinking/linking** situation from sections 2.2.8.3 and 2.2.8.4, and is where **Ctrl+Z** comes in handy).

2.4.2. Section Breaks

Another common use of the section break is to change the page orientation. Remember, **page breaks insert a new page, but don't allow us to change the page formatting**; only section breaks allow us this functionality. So, if we want to change from portrait to landscape we need one section break, and if we want to change it back again afterwards, we'll need a second.

2.4.3. How Can We See Section Breaks (and All That Other Stuff)?

Before we do this, as section breaks are hidden, it's difficult to know what's going on with, or in, a Word document when you view your document without the hidden characters turned on. So to avoid error (and if you didn't turn them on earlier), it's always best to turn **Show/Hide** [characters] on. To do this:

1.   Click on **Home** on the menu bar.

2.   Click on the **Show/Hide** button.

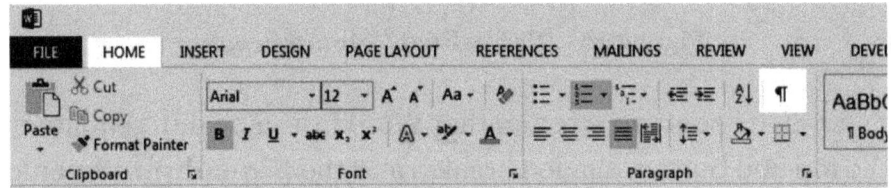

Figure 28 - Show/Hide Button

Alternatively, and as mentioned briefly in section 2.4.1, you can press **Ctrl+Shift+8** on your keyboard.

Now we've turned on **Show/Hide** (it's a toggle option, so click on it again to turn it off), I can add my section breaks and change the next page to landscape.

This is what we see. I have highlighted the **next page** section breaks in the image above (on the portrait page to change the next page formatting to whatever I require, in this case to landscape), and below the image (on the landscape page still, to change the next page formatting, also to whatever I require, but in this case is back to portrait to continue my document flow - refer to Figure 29)[3]:

Note: you can turn these on permanently in Word's global options (**File** > **Options** > **Display**), but I prefer to **Ctrl+Shift+8** as and when I require it.

---

[3] I don't have to change the page orientation, what is key here is the breaks allow me to change the formatting to whatever I want and it **will not** affect the previous section; so, if I wanted, I could change the page size, the margin size, the page color, anything I like. It's just that page orientation is probably the most common.

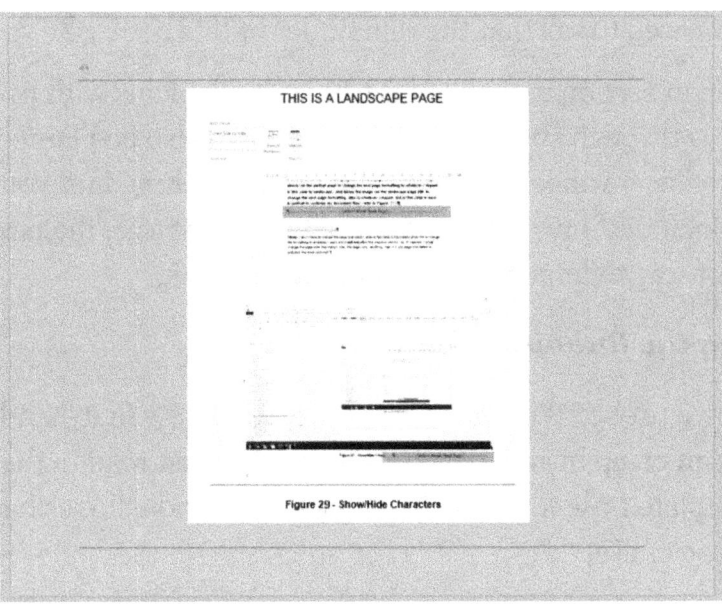

Figure 29 - Show/Hide Characters[4]

Then, with the second section break, we can revert back to portrait.

As mentioned, the section break allows us to modify the format of the section.

You wouldn't have noticed the page number on the landscape page, but I'd changed it to Thai numbers: this is another function of the section break in that it allows us to change the page number type, their formatting, numbering, etc.

If you notice the chapter names in the headers on the odd-numbered pages in this book, you couldn't do this with a page break. To do so would only leave you with a single section, and the way Word works is that the contents of that header and footer would replicate through the entire document—you must use section breaks.

I admit that this can sound confusing and probably a bit above the level of many Word users, but I hope you're getting a clearer understanding of the intricacies of the way Word works. It's a fact though, they can be confusing and can take some getting used to.

---

[4] **Note**: CreateSpace won't allow me to use a landscape page, so I've had to take an image of the landscape page and insert it in the portrait page.

However, I'm pleased to say that the remainder of this book gets so much easier.

As I emphasized in section 2.3, one of the biggest problems with people using Word correctly is through styles, but Word itself can also be blamed, as unless you tell it otherwise, it will let you copy and paste anything into your document or book; and this includes unwanted styles. So, to prevent this, the next section explains the best way to import material into your book.

2.4.4. Keeping the Rubbish Away

If you have been a user of Word for some time, you know first-hand some of the problems that can creep in and, despite what you've just read in the previous section, the template I use for my CreateSpace and Kindle books has been set up primarily for ease of use.

If you use the **styles** setup in the template (modify them as you see fit) and keep all other external styles away, then you've got a greater chance of preserving your/the template.

However, Word will let you bring in whatever styles you want and, if you do, it'll then do the best it can to figure out what you've got and what you're trying to do; then, it will then act in what it thinks are its best interests to do what needs to be done.

The chances are though, in my experience, what it wants and what you want are unlikely to be in-sync, and it's unlikely that the end result will either be a success, or even close to it.

So, don't risk it, sanitize your text first.

Sanitizing does add a little to the time it takes to format your book, but trust me you'll save yourself a lot of time in the long run.

2.4.4.1. Sanitizing Your Document

There are a number of ways to sanitize your document, but the easiest and safest way is to run it through Notepad. If you've used Word before and have a different method, then by all means use that; however, if you don't, or are unsure, I would recommend Notepad. All you need to do is:

1. Open **Notepad** on your computer.

2. Open your document\book in whatever application it's been written in.

3. Copy the first page, chapter, or whatever you think is acceptable to try this process out—you can include headings; **Ctrl+C** is the quickest way: hold down the **Ctrl** key on your keyboard and then press **C**.

4. Switch across to Notepad, and paste your selection into a blank page (use **Ctrl+V** to paste).

Your selection is now sanitized in Notepad and can go into Word.

I know when you paste from Notepad into Word, your headings and everything will look the same, but formatting in Word is so fast that it won't matter. The idea of this process is to clear out all your old styles.

1. Select the text in Notepad (**Ctrl+A** will **Select All**).

2. Copy it (**Ctrl+C**).

3. Switch over to your Word document (**Alt+Tab** key), to Chapter 1. Put your cursor in the body text where you want to insert your text.

The best place is to insert it in a **Body style** paragraph. **DO NOT put the cursor in/where a heading is**. Before you paste, delete any text on that line so that only the cursor remains.

---

4. Then, **Ctrl+V** (paste) your information in.

5. Go back to your original document, and select the next part (or you could even **Select All**, using **Ctrl+A**).

6. Copy it (**Ctrl+C**).

7. Switch to **Notepad.**

8. **Ctrl+V** (paste) into Notepad.

9. **Ctrl+C** (copy) the text in Notepad.

10. Switch to Word, **Ctrl+V** paste it in, etc.

Rinse-and-repeat (this means do the same thing again and again) until your entire document is pasted into the Word template as **Body** style. If it takes you a while to do this, then that's life. If you **Select All** and then paste it in like that, it takes seconds. The important point is that our template/book is "clean", and we can now work with the text.

2.5.   Formatting Your Document

By reading this far, you now know that I'm obsessed by styles; but, as you're about to find out, I'm also a convert and utterly dedicated to using shortcuts.

I will go on record as saying that I am a firm believer in doing things right, but I'm also an ardent supporter of doing them efficiently. Now, this doesn't mean I rush things, far from it, it's just that though there's very often a right way and a wrong way to do something, there's also very often a quick way and a slow way.

With styles, there are actually three ways you can format your document. Personally, I prefer the quick way, but I'll show you all three; first, the slowest method.

2.5.1. *The Slow Method*

The slow method of formatting your document is by using the styles one at a time; so:

1. Click in the paragraph you wish to format to select it, e.g. your first Heading 1 (it's a paragraph style so don't select any text).

2. Move your mouse up to the style ribbon.

3. Click on the style you want to apply, e.g. Heading 1.

4. The style will be applied.

Remember, the vast majority of your document will be **Body** style and, as it's already been pasted in as this style, you should only have to format a small part of your document.

Next we'll look at the slightly faster method...

2.5.2. The Quicker Method

The quicker way uses **format painter**.

Now, in my experience (and despite it being in plain view) few have heard of **format painter**. It's crazy, but I guess that's also a fault of the designers in that they put so much clutter in the User Interface (UI) that it's almost as if we suffer "button-blindness."

Anyway, it's there, it's always been there, and it's ready to be used.

1.   Click on **Home,** and there she is:

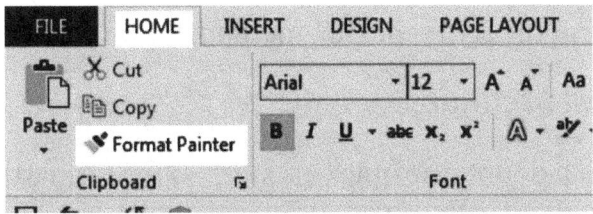

Figure 30 - Format Painter

Format painter allows you to copy the formatting from a paragraph (or, in the case of a character style, a selection of text) and to apply that same style to other parts of your document. It's almost as if you're taking paint from a single tin and applying it to your wall—it all then looks the same.

2.   Place your cursor in the paragraph of the format you want to replicate, e.g. in a Heading 1 title—Heading 1 is the best place to start.

3.   Double-click on the "**Format Painter**" button (if you single-click, it will only let you apply the formatting once). When you have **Format Painter** selected, your cursor will change to: 🖌️ when it's hovered over your page.

4.   Then, by using the **Page Up** and **Page Down** buttons on your keyboard, you can quickly go through your document and format all Heading 1's.

5.   If you have the Navigation pane visible on the left, you will see your document start to come together (click on **View** on the menu bar, then on **Navigation Pane** (in **Show**) to toggle it on and off).

6. Once you've finished your Heading 1's, you can go and format Heading 2's, 3's, then bulleted lists, numbered lists, and the remainder of your document.

    You should be able to do this very quickly.

To cancel **Format Painter** at any time, press the **Esc** key on your keyboard.

Note: if you try and type or do some other mouse or keyboard function while **Format Painter** is in operation, it will most likely cancel the formatting operation and you'll need to start again from the last selection point.

As you can see, though you format your document according to similar chunks, this is far quicker than the style-clicking method.

2.5.3. The Quickest Method

Without a shadow of a doubt, the quickest method for formatting a Word document is by using the keyboard. Using either of the previous 2 options requires you to use the mouse and, by its very nature, moving it about and having to be precise with your clicking takes longer.

However, if you use the keyboard for all your typing and your formatting, then your fingers never need to leave the keyboard.

Word has a number of default shortcut keys setup, and if you want to print these out and get to grips with them:

1. Click on **File**

2. Click on **Print**

3. In **Settings**, click on the drop-down arrow and select **Key Assignments.**

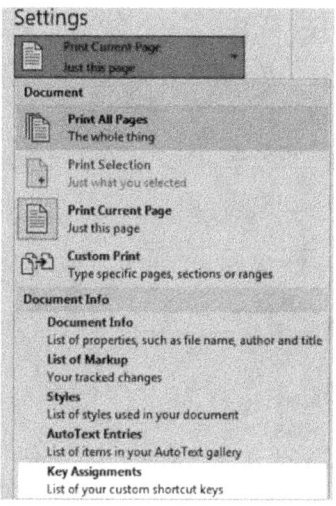

Figure 31 - Print Key Assignments

4.   Click on **Print**

There are a lot of them (and you can't print out part of this list either).

In the 1CBC Template, the following style shortcuts are used:

- Headings:
    - Heading 1—**Ctrl+1**
    - Heading 2—**Ctrl+2**
    - Heading 3—**Ctrl+3**
    - Heading 4—**Ctrl+4**
- Numbers:
    - Numbers Level 1—**Alt+N,1**
    - Numbers Level 2—**Alt+N,2**
    - Numbers Level 3—**Alt+N,3**
    - Numbers Level 4—**Alt+N,4**
- Bullets
    - Bullets Level 1—**Alt+B,1**

- – Bullets Level 2—**Alt+B,2**
- – Bullets Level 3—**Alt+B,3**
- – Bullets Level 4—**Alt+B,4**
- Indented Text
- – Indent Level 1—**Alt+I,1**
- – Indent Level 2—**Alt+I,2**
- – Indent Level 3—**Alt+I,3**
- – Indent Level 4—**Alt+I,4**
- Body Text—**Alt+B,T**
- FirstPara—**Alt+F,P**
- Graphic style—**Alt+G,R**
- Important—**Alt+I,M**
- Quote—**Alt+Q,T**
- Intense Quote—**Alt+I,Q**

The above styles and shortcut keys comprise the vast majority of the styles I [ever] use in the template. I have one or two other styles defined for each specific book I author; for example, the 'Answers' below use an 'Answer' style, configured specifically for this book.

Of course, learning these shortcuts doesn't really do you much good if you're still navigating with the mouse, wearing out your fingers by pressing the arrow keys repeatedly, or even using the Page Up/Down buttons; so, the best way is to learn to use the keyboard as well.

2.6. Navigating Using the Keyboard

You no doubt already know about navigating with the mouse or how to use the Page Up or Page Down keys, so I'll ask you a question:

*Question: what happens if you press the **Left arrow** (←) or the **Right arrow** (→) on your keyboard?*

Answer: Your cursor moves one **character** to the left, or one **character** to the right.

*Question: what happens if you hold down the **Ctrl** key and then press the **Left** arrow (←) or the **Right arrow** (→) on your keyboard?*

Answer: Your cursor moves one **word** to the left, or one **word** to the right.

*Question: what happens if you press **Home** key, or the **end** key when your cursor is on a line?*

Answer: Your cursor moves to the **start** or to the **end** of the line.

Question: what happens if you press the Up arrow (↑) or the Down arrow (↓) on your keyboard?

Answer: Your cursor moves one **line** up, or one **line** down. I think you'll agree, that's quite handy.

*Question: what happens if you hold down the **Ctrl** key and then press the Up arrow (↑) or the Down arrow (↓) on your keyboard?*

Answer: Your cursor moves one **paragraph** up, or one **paragraph** down. Now, that's **very** handy!

Though you don't need it to format paragraphs, I'll leave it to you to figure out what happens if you **also** press the **Shift** key **with** the above keystrokes.

Do you now see how, with a combination of quick keys for styles and quick keys for navigation, your productivity levels have just become super-charged?

Now you can either go through and format your entire book or, if you're currently writing it, format it quickly and efficiently as you go.

Note: section 2.7 applies to the full 1-Click Book Creation Template only, and not to the free download. The full version is a macro-enabled template, which allows me to automate many functions to help you.

Unfortunately, many shy away from macros as they can contain nasty code, but with the full version, I have a signed security certificate, created by me, which guarantees the code is safe. This is only accessible within a secure area and this ensures its integrity.

If I allowed this certificate out of a secure area, anyone could theoretically tamper with it, and I would have no control. So, have a look at the extra functionality offered, and if you feel this may simplify things, be of use to you, and save you an enormous amount of time (it will), then head over to www.1clickbookcreation.com.

2.7.   Toolbars

I've also added two toolbars to aid you: **YOUR BOOK** and **MAIN STYLES**.

The menus have been used to bring all the most common tasks you'll need to perform into a central area. At first glance, with its myriad of buttons and so much unknown functionality, the Word interface looks so daunting; but, as is often the case, you'll only actually use the core features, the rest are just window-dressing: it is these core elements that I've put into these menus.

2.7.1. *Your Book Menu*

The **YOUR BOOK** menu is as shown in Figure 32:

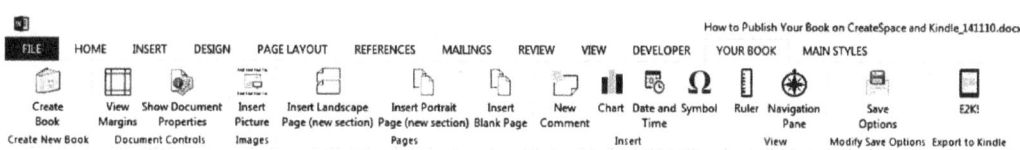

Figure 32 - Your Book Menu

As you can see, from the left we have:

- **Create Book**—displays the start-up form, and allows you to create a new book. This can only be run from the main template, not from a book that's already been created.

- **View Margins**—if you need to modify your margins, or your page setup.

- **Show Document Properties**—the attributes and properties information for your current document.

- **Insert Picture**—this will insert a picture with text top and bottom, as I have done in this book.

- **Insert Landscape Page** (**New section**)—no need to worry about section breaks, just click here to add a new landscape page.

- **Insert Portrait Page** (**New Section**)—same as above, but it inserts a portrait page.

- **Insert Blank Page**—inserts a page break at your cursor.

- **New Comment**—it's always nice to leave yourself a comment or a reminder once in a while, especially during research or editing.

- **Chart**—insert a chart at the cursor point.

- **Date and Time**—insert the date and time.

- **Symbol**—I use the symbol palette all the time, so it's nice to have it handy.

- **Ruler**—this is indispensable when working with documents, styles (and troubleshooting).

- **Navigation Pane**—not only does it let you see the layout, structure, and flow of your document, but it's also offers 1-click navigation to any heading.

- **Save Options**—many people forget to save their documents and even though they work on it for months, still use the same single doc. This option gives you different choices, including to autosave each new day.

- **E2K**—this performs a Kindle clean-up of your document (removes extra spaces, paragraph marks, etc.) and saves your book for Kindle in the Hypertext Mark-up Language (HTML) format.

I was going to write about what each of these do, but one of the things with learning Word is working out what each of the parts do. All you need to do is remember the **Ctrl+Z** (Undo) shortcut and you can click away. Alternatively, you can refer to the tooltips (section 2.7.3).

2.7.2. Main Styles Menu

As mentioned earlier, this menu brings most of the common functionality into one area for you. If you use the mouse a lot, it makes it easier for you. The Main Styles menu is shown in Figure 33:

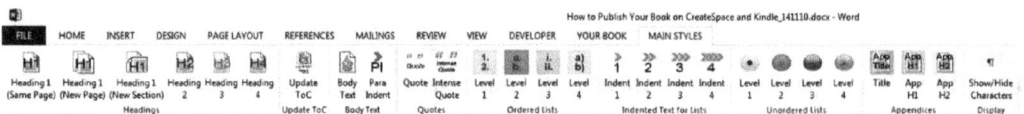

Figure 33 - Main Styles Menu

From the left, we have the Headings section, which though I'll explain this next, there isn't any need to elaborate on the functionality of the other items, as all they do is apply the set style to wherever your cursor is positioned.

As you can see, there are three Heading 1 options:

- **Heading 1 (Same Page)**—inserts a new Heading 1 at your cursor.

- **Heading 1 (New Page)**—inserts a page break at your cursor and inserts a Heading 1 at the top of the next page.

- **Heading 1** (**New Section**)—inserts a next page section break at your cursor, and inserts a Heading 1 at the top of the next page.

2.7.3. Tooltips

One of the advantages of adding new menu bars to the interface is that it allows you to write your own tooltips and provide [perhaps] more relevant information. Just hover your mouse cursor over any of the buttons and you'll not only be reminded of the function of the button, but also be reminded of the shortcut key to apply this style:

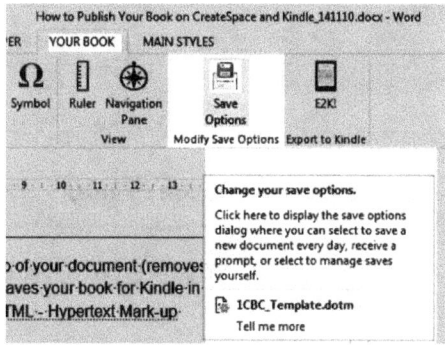

Figure 34 - Tooltip

2.8.   Updating Your Table of Contents

Once your book is formatted correctly, the Heading 1's, Heading 2's, etc., you can update your ToC.

Within the template, the ToC, the Index of Figures, Index of Tables, and Abbreviations use what are called *field codes*, little snippets of code that Word uses to automate certain information types. All you need to do is to enter your information/content correctly and then just update the field codes.

There are two simple ways that you can update your ToC, your Abbreviations, Index of Tables, or Index of Figures within Word:

- Method 1:
    a. Use **Ctrl+A** (to **Select All**).

b. Press **F9.**

Note: this updates **all fields** in your document.

- Method 2:

    a. Place your cursor in the respective table field.

    b. Right-click and select **Update Field:**

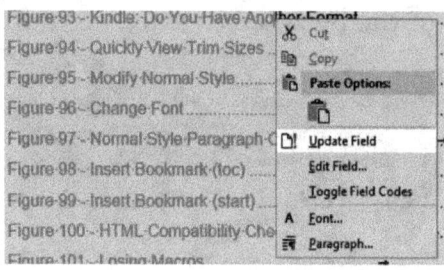

Figure 35 - Update Field

c. Then, select either **Update Page Numbers Only** or **Update Entire Table**:

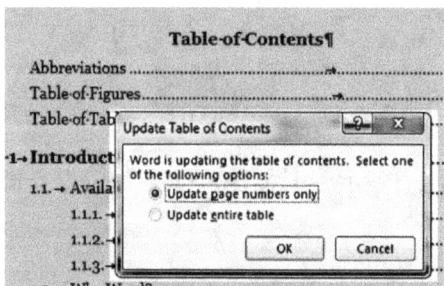

Figure 36 - Update ToC Options

The table field will then update.

2.9.   Index of Tables, Figures, and Abbreviations

If you require these for your book, then we have to take your learning just a little bit further. As with the ToC we mentioned earlier, the information on this page also uses field codes. Naturally, you don't update these manually. You enter the required information in your book in the correct manner, and then you update these fields that are "looking" for your document entries.

If you look at the page for the indexes, you can see that the template itself inserts the individual "container" code for each of these indexes, so you don't have to.

Right-click on any of the fields and select **Toggle Field Codes**:

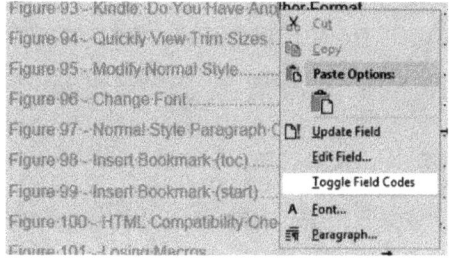

Figure 37 - Toggle Field Codes

You will see:

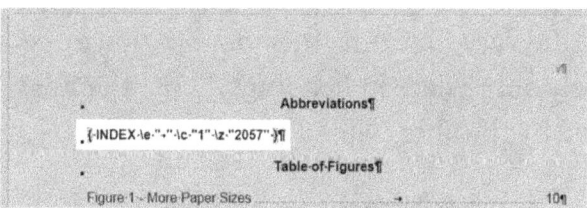

Figure 38 - Viewing Field Codes

If you don't require these items in your document, then you can just delete them from the page. For example, if you only require the **Index of Tables** and the **Index of Figures**, just select the **Abbreviations** and the line of code beneath it and delete it:

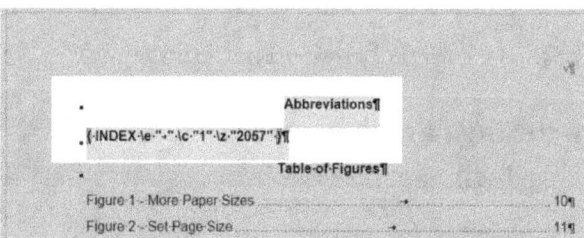

Figure 39 - Delete Unwanted Field Codes

So, as you can see, this is an easy way of managing these information types. But for the field codes to pick up the required information from your book, the information needs to be entered correctly.

2.9.1. Adding Index Items Correctly

We use two different methods of entering this information in our books: abbreviations and indexes. We'll look at Abbreviations first.

2.9.1.1. Abbreviations

As with all our Word work-methods, there's usually a slow way and a quick way; and, though we'll look at the slow way first, a short word on the convention I use for Abbreviations.

Regardless of the convention you prefer, as in all documentation, it pays to be consistent in usage, so don't mix-and-match.

The one I use is that the very first time the abbreviation appears in the body of the document (I rarely abbreviate in headings), I list the full term, followed by a single space, followed by the abbreviated term in brackets/parentheses. So:

full term (Abb frm*)

* Abb frm = abbreviated form, e.g. **Table of Contents (ToC).**

Thereafter, you use the abbreviation itself: **ToC**.

Then, when I index the item, I use the abbreviated term first, then a space, then a hyphen, then another space, followed by the full term: almost a reverse of the in-text indexed entry, as this is what will appear in my index:

Abb frm – full term

So, the first time that the item I wish to mark appears in the document, I will select the text entry that I will mark as the index:

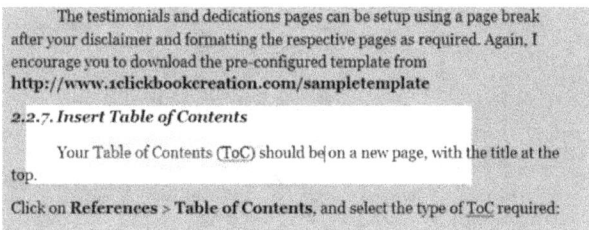

Figure 40 - Marking an Abbreviation

Then I can add this in one of two ways, with the mouse or the keyboard.

2.9.1.2. Using the Mouse (Slow Method)

1. Select the word that you wish to abbreviate. As Figure 41 shows, you don't need to select the abbreviated form, just the full term:

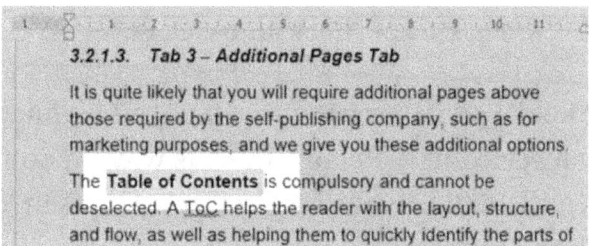

Figure 41 - Select the Text to Mark

2. Click on **References** on the menu bar.

3. Then click on **Mark Entry**. If the text in the document is bold, the entry in the dialog box will also be bold. Press **Ctrl+B** to remove the bold formatting:

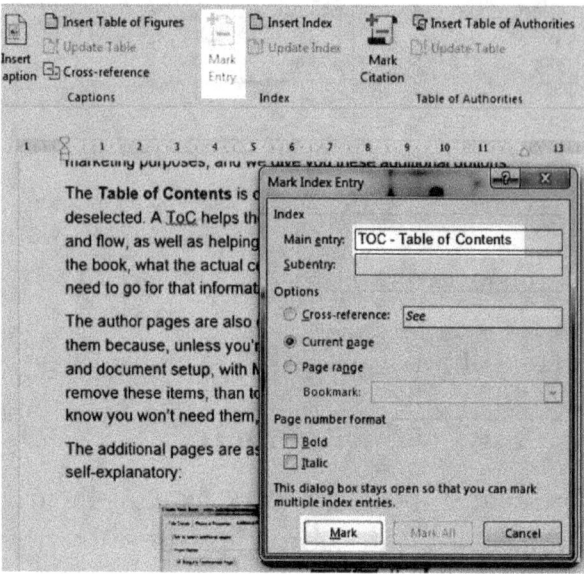

Figure 42 - Mark an Index Entry

In the **Main Entry** field, you will see that the text you highlighted in your document is already inserted in the field (which is why we don't want to select the abbreviated form as well). All you need to do is move the cursor to the front of the text and insert the remainder.

You can enter a sub-entry and cross-reference and all the other options on the dialog form, but they're out of the scope of this tutorial. These are fully covered in our other Word training courses.

4.   Click on the **Mark** button to mark that entry in your document.

      Word will default to showing you the field code that it uses for marking an index entry:

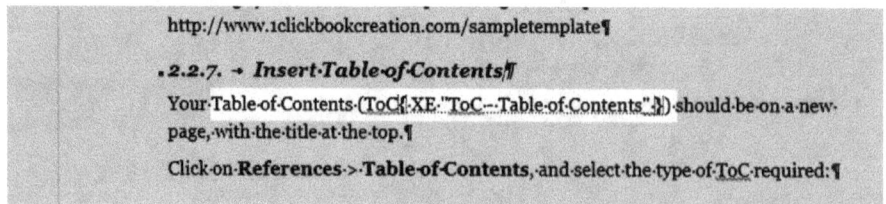

Figure 43 - Index Entry Marked

1.   To turn the **Show/Hide** characters off, press **Ctrl-Shift-8**.

2.   Go to your abbreviation field code, right-click on it, and select **Update Field** to update your Index of Abbreviations:

Abbreviations

Figure 44 - Index Updated

Note: I would advise **against** clicking on the **Mark All** button when indexing, as this will mark every instance of the entry in the document. As a rule, I only mark the very first entry in the document.

Next, we'll look at a much faster method of indexing an entry.

2.9.1.3.   *Using the Keyboard (Quick Method)*

1.   Select the text that you wish to mark as an index entry (as shown in Figure 41).

2.   Press **Alt-Shift-X**.

3.   Click **Mark**.

That's it. That way much easier, wasn't it?

Now, we'll move onto how we mark entries for our **Index of Tables** and **Index of Figures**.

2.9.2. *Index of Tables and Index of Figures*

These two both use the same method for marking, whether as a table or as a figure. The actual term we use in these cases is **Insert Caption**.

Unlike adding an index entry for an abbreviation, the quickest way to insert a caption is to continue using the mouse.

2.9.2.1.   *Insert Caption – Tables*

When selecting a table to mark, you need to:

1.   Click in the table, or select the entire table (by mousing-over the table) until the selection handle in the top left appears:

Figure 45 - Table Selection Handle

2.   Right-click on the selection handle to display the drop-down list:

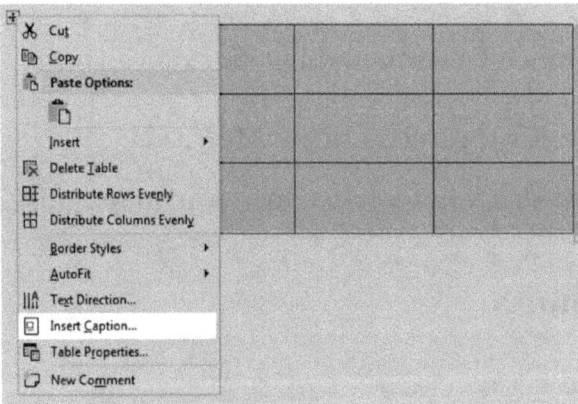

Figure 46 - Insert Caption (Table)

3.   Select **Insert Caption**. The **Caption** dialog box will display:

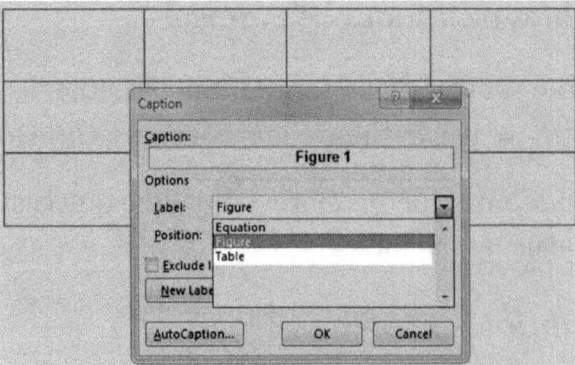

Figure 47 - Change Label

4.   By default, the caption type is set to **Figure**. You need to click on the **Label** drop-down and select **Table** (as shown in Figure 46).

5.   In the **Caption** field, enter your caption. I always enter a space, then a hyphen, then the caption (this is similar to the format I use for abbreviations), as shown in Figure 48:

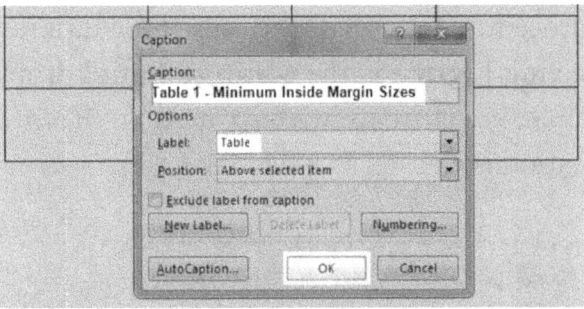

Figure 48 - Enter Caption Title

6.   Select the **position** for your caption to go. Some conventions, such as the American Psychological Society (APA) style, require table captions above the table, whereas figure captions go below the figure.

7.   Press **Ok**.

Table·1·-·Minimum·Inside·Margin·Sizes¶

Page·Count¤	Minimum·Inside·Margin¤
24–150·¤	0.375"¤
151–400¤	0.75"¤
401–600¤	0.875"¤
>600¤	1.0"¤

Figure 49 - Finished Table

8.   Your caption will be inserted (refer to Figure 49).

9.   Next, go to the page where your index of tables is, right-click in the field and select **Update Field** from the drop-down list (as shown in Figure 35). Your **Index of Tables** will update:

Table of Tables

Figure 50 - Index of Tables Updated

2.9.2.2. *Insert Caption – Figures*

If you followed the procedure in 2.9.2.1, the only thing different when inserting a figure caption is selecting **Figure** in the **Change Label** drop-down (as shown in Figure 47). For example, in Figure 51, we have an image (**Note:** anything that is not a table or an equation is classed as a figure):

Figure 51 – New Figure

1.   Single left click on the figure to select it:

Figure 52 - Select Figure

2.   Right-click on the figure and select **Insert Caption**:

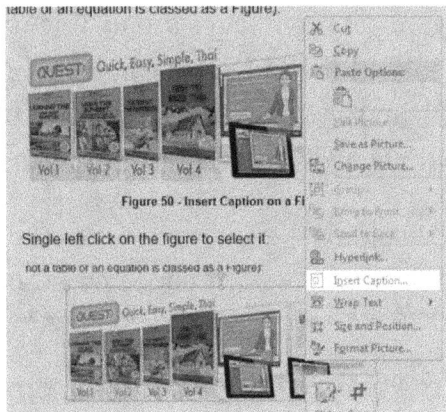

Figure 53 - Insert Caption (Figure)

3. Repeat steps 5-8 from the previous procedure.

4. Update your **Table of Figures** by right-clicking in it and selecting **Update Field** (as shown in Figure 35).

That's how you create and update indexes and abbreviations and which will, of course, need to be updated as you add to or modify your document (remember, you can also do **Ctrl+A**, to **Select All** in your book, and can then press the **F9** key to update all fields).

2.10. Inserting Pictures

When you insert pictures into your book, it's important that you insert them using the Word **Insert Picture** functionality, otherwise Word is apt to do its own thing and recompress you images as it sees fit; and, this isn't good for either a print version of your book, or for a Kindle version.

The two main methods for inserting pictures are with what are called **Inline with text**, and **Floating**. All the images in this book use the former; and, unless there's a compelling reason for you to do otherwise, I'd recommend that. If you do the latter, then you have to be conscious that as you add more text and pictures to your book, this may affect the on-page layout, and your text and images will likely move.

Hopefully, all will be okay, but if the images are in-line with text, you know they will be. Besides, if your book is for Kindle, they have to be in-line with text. If it's for a printed copy, then it's up to you where or how you place them, as long as the images are 300 dpi (or, with Word's image limitations, 220 dpi).

This is important for Kindle, your images **must** be inline with text.

We have placed the **Insert Picture** button on the **Your Book** menu (in the fully licensed version only), and it will insert as **in-line** with text by default using the pre-configured '**Graphic**' style; however, if you don't have this or you want to make the image floating (or any of the other floating-type formats), it's simple to do:

1. Single-click on the image to select it.

2. Right-click and mouseover **Wrap text**:

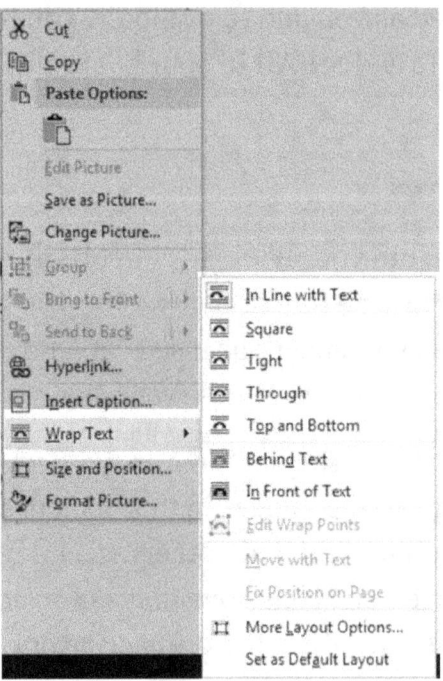

Figure 54 - Picture Wrap Text Options

Now, you can select either **Square**, **Tight**, **Through**, **Top-and-bottom**, **Behind Text**, or **In Front of Text**.

Note: These are pretty self-explanatory, but I'd recommend playing about with the settings to obtain a feel for each.

3. Once you've selected the text-wrapping option, you can move the image and position it as required.

4. In the left margin, you will see an anchor:

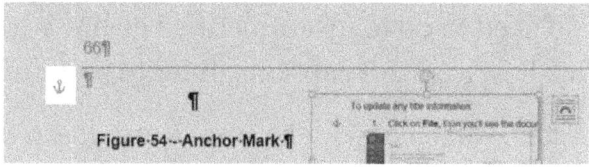

Figure 55 - Anchor Mark

5. Left-click on the anchor and drag it to the paragraph you wish to anchor this image to.

6. Then, if you wish to lock the anchor to that text, right-click on the image, and select **Size and Position**.

7. In the dialog box, click on the **Position** tab.

8. Click on **Lock Anchor**:

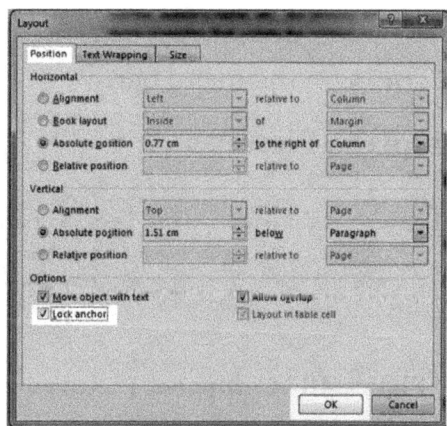

Figure 56 - Lock Anchor

9. Click on **Ok**. The anchor will be locked to that paragraph:

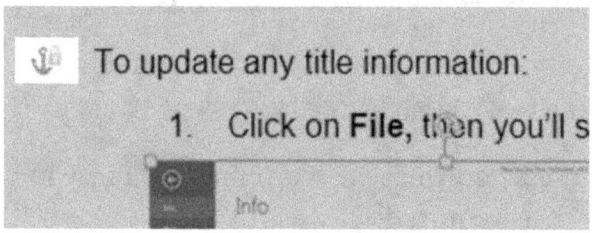

Figure 57 - Locked Anchor

That's it. That's all you need to do to insert pictures in-line with text and as floating images. To see how to insert captions, refer to section 2.9.2.1 or 2.9.2.2.

Now that they're inserted, we need to make sure Word doesn't screw them up.

2.10.1.   DPI Settings

Your images need to be at least 200 dpi for a printed book; but I would advise you to go for at least 300 dpi. Word will reduce them to 220 dpi, but if you decide later to use the images elsewhere, you still have them at 300 dpi.

We did already set this in the Word options back in section 2.1, but sometimes Word will do its own thing so, before you finalize your document and export it to off, ensure you do the following:

1. With any image in your book, left-click to select the first image in your book.

2. Click on **Picture Tools** on the menu bar.

3. Then click on **Compress Pictures**:

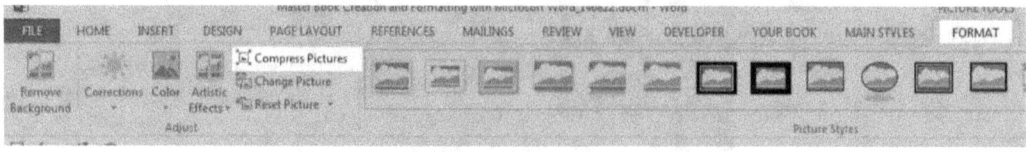

Figure 58 - Compress Pictures

4. Then, in the **Compress Pictures** dialog box:

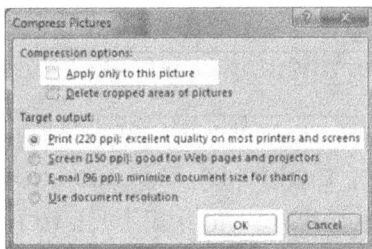

Figure 59 - Compress Picture Options

5.   Deselect, **Apply only to this Picture**.

6.   Select, **Print (220 dpi)...**

7.   Click **Ok**.

That's it, your pictures will be at the best resolution that Word will allow.

Hopefully, following all we've covered in this section will enable you to set-up and format your book professionally. If you do need some assistance, head over to www.red-dragon-publishing.com and get in touch.

2.11.   Finalizing and Reviewing Your Book

When I've finished writing my work, whether it is a book, an article, or whatever, I always go through at least three proofreads of my own.

1st Draft

1.   When I first sit down to write, I put anything on paper (or the screen in this case) as it's just my draft copy: no-one but me gets to read it, so it doesn't matter what I say or write (or even that it makes 100% sense).

2.   When I've finished my 1st draft, I go through (proof it) quickly on my PC to look for errors and a tidy-up. It needs to be readable and make sense.

3.   Then I export it to .pdf (refer to section 2.12) and import it into **Goodreads** on my iPad. I then proof it for the 2nd time on my iPad (still as part of my 1st draft).

2nd Draft

4. Here I go through it word-by-word, line-by-line. In terms of proofing/editing, it is this stage that takes me the longest.

    If it's just a typo, I can mark it with my iPad pen; if I want to change chunks, I use the type facility as that then allows me to copy and paste what I've written from the .pdf back to the Word document when I update it (and saves me a lot of time).

5. After the .pdf is edited in Goodreads, I email that back to me and open it on my PC. I then update the Word document with all the changes.

    Once I've made the changes in the Word document, I make sure that everything is 100%: layout, formatting, updated ToC's, figures, tables—everything. This is now close to where I want.

3rd Draft

6. Once that's complete and I'm happy with the work, I print it out double-sided and let it sit for as long as I can (or as long as I am able to). Then, I start to read it out loud, marking up as I go.

    By the time I've finished this 3rd draft, the book is almost ready to go to my editor; but, first, I need to update any modifications or changes out of this section.

7. Then, I send it to my editor for their review and comments.

8. On its return, the book is updated accordingly and will either go back for another review or it undergoes a final check before publishing.

That's the general process I go through, but very often the 2nd and 3rd draft steps may be repeated, depending on the work itself. I would recommend that you do something similar as proofing and editing can make or break your book. I list a number of important steps/activities concerning proofing and editing your work in Appendix C.

2.12. Export to PDF

Exporting to .pdf is simple with Word:

1. Click on **File.**

2.   Click on **Export.**

3.   Click on the **Create PDF/XPS** button. The following dialog will display:

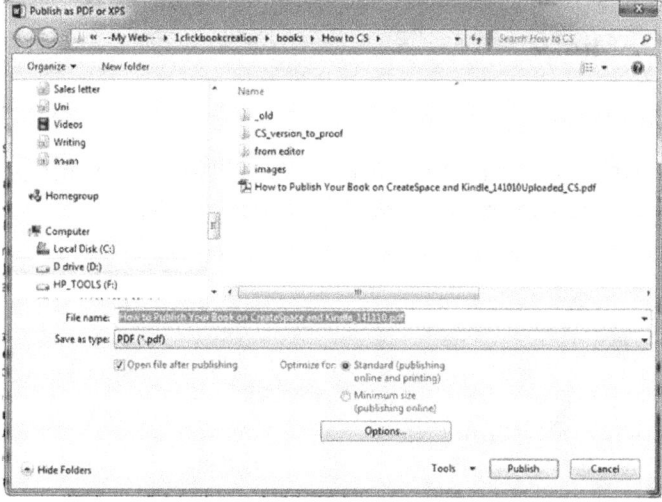

Figure 60 - Export as PDF

4.   Ensure **Standard Publishing** is selected.

5.   Click on the **Options** button. The following will display:

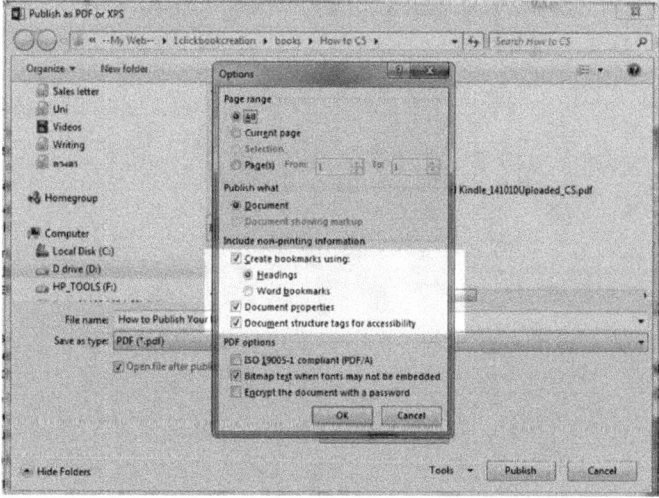

Figure 61 - Select Options

6.   Ensure that **Create bookmarks using > Headings** is selected, as this will create the appropriate navigation in your .pdf document.

7.   Click on **Ok.**

8.   Click on **Publish**.

Your .pdf will be created.

Regardless of the number of times you have read through your book in the review process above, always check the .pdf before uploading it to CreateSpace—always!

Just in case.

3. Publishing to CreateSpace

Publishing to CreateSpace is both easy and free. All you need is a web-browser and an Internet connection. You can set your account up at any time, and can come back to it anytime you want.

Now you've formatted your book, you will have proofed and edited it, and it is now ready for publication. If you wish, you can set-up your project—your book is a project in CreateSpace—well in advance, but until you submit your book files (interior file and cover file), you can only progress so far.

In this section, we will cover the simple steps to publishing to CreateSpace, how to setup an account, and create a new project. Then we will walk you step-by-step through the entire process.

To illustrate this, I will be publishing this actual book via CreateSpace and Kindle.

This book was created using the 1-Click Book Creation template available from:

http://www.1clickbookcreation.com

Full video training of how I created this book, from start-to-finish, is also available on the website.

3.1.   Simple Steps to Publishing on CreateSpace

There are five main steps and a number of sub-steps to publishing your book:

1.   **Create an Account**

2.   **Setup Your Book**, including:

   a. Title Information

   b. ISBN

   c. Interior

   d. Cover

   e. Complete Setup.

3.   **Review**, which involves:

   a. File Review

   b. Proof Your Book.

4.   **Distribute**:

   a. Channels

   b. Pricing

   c. Cover Finish

   d. Description

   e. Publish on Kindle.

5.   **Sales & Marketing**, including advice on Tracking Sales, Marketing Services

To get started though, you need to register with CreateSpace, and that means creating an account.

3.2.   Create an Account

To create an account, carry out the following:

1. Open your preferred web browser (mine is Firefox) and go to: http://www.createspace.com. You will see:

Figure 62 - CreateSpace Homepage

2. Click on the **Sign-up** button The following will display:

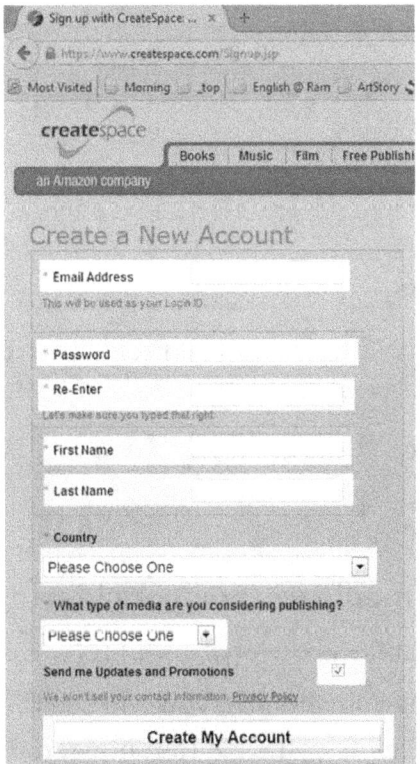

Figure 63 - Create a New Account

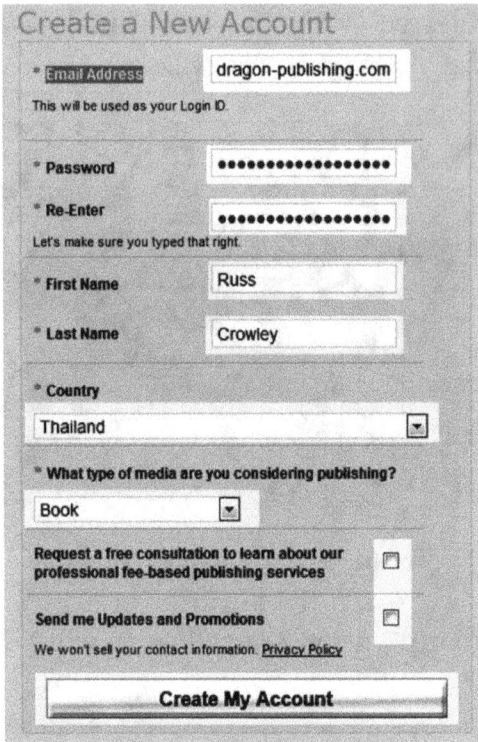

Figure 64 - Details Entered

3.   Populate the form with your required details. You will need the following information:

   – **Email Address**

   – **Password** (you will need to re-enter this to confirm it)

   – **First name**

   – **Last name**

   – **Country**

   – **What type of media are you considering publishing?**

   Note: all the fields are required, and if you select **book** in the type of media option (as you should), you will see the two additional options. Make your choices as you wish (as shown in Figure 64).

4.   Click on **Create My Account**.

5. The screen will refresh, and while you are waiting for your verification
    email to be delivered at the email address you specified above, you will be
    presented with the Services Agreement which you need to agree to:

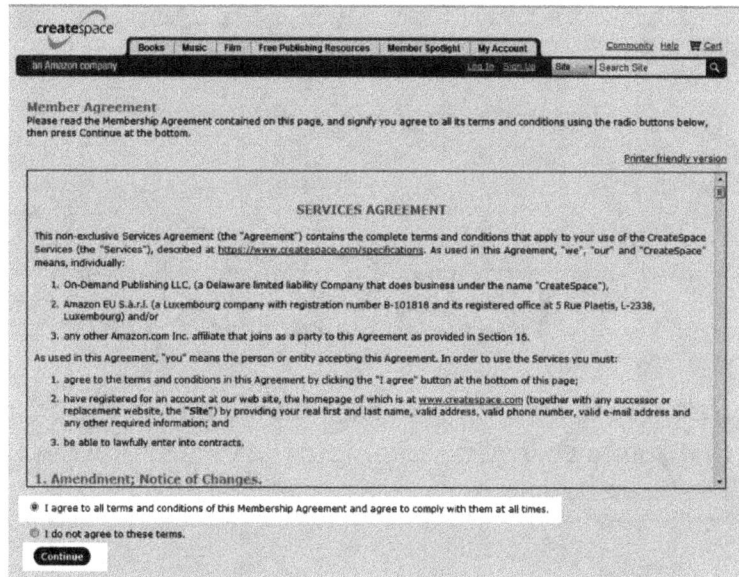

Figure 65 - Accepting the Services Agreement

6. Click on **Continue**.

7. The screen will refresh and you will be presented with the **Verify Your
    Email Address** screen:

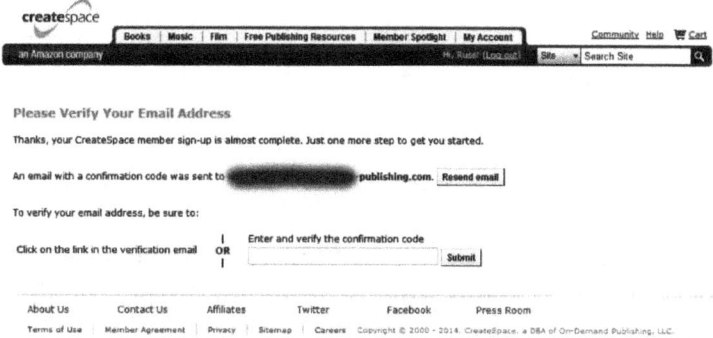

Figure 66 - Verify Email Address

8. Now, switch to your email account and open the required email.

If the email has not arrived, you can click on the **Resend email button** in your browser page. You can only do this once every 15 minutes though.

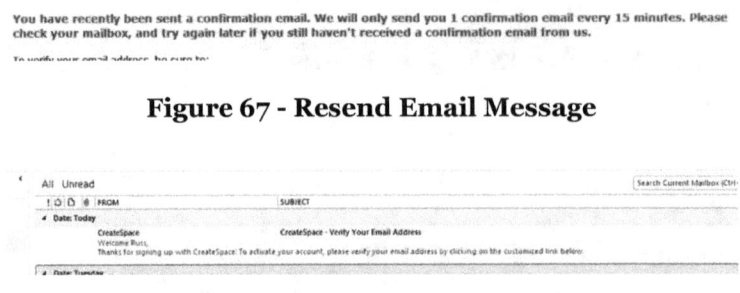

Figure 67 - Resend Email Message

Figure 68 - Email Arrived

9.   The easiest way to confirm is to click on the link in the email, but there is a code that you can copy and enter into the verification field in the browser page:

Figure 69 - Confirm Email Address

10.   Then, the screen will refresh, and you will see the following image telling you that your account has now been created (plus you'll receive this in-your-face attempt at getting you to avail yourself of their services):

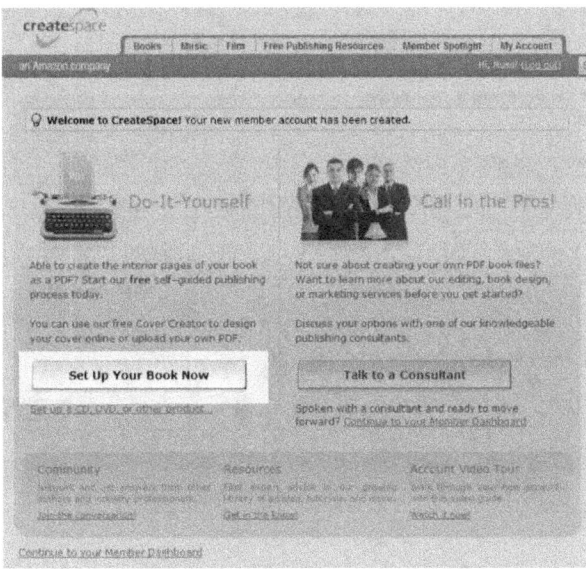

Figure 70 - Account Created

11. You can click on **Continue to your Member Dashboard** (the bottom left), but as we're here to setup our first book, we'll do that now: click on the **Setup Your Book Now** button.

3.3. Setup Your Book

Now we will look at setting up your new book. There are five sub-steps to this part of the process: 1) **Title Information**; 2) **ISBN**; 3) **Interior**; 4) **Cover**; and, 5) **Complete Setup**.

On each page is a **Save** and a **Save & Continue** button. Using these means you don't ever need to lose your information and you can enter as little, or as much information as required. Additionally, you can then leave it, returning whenever you want to.

We'll start by creating our new project.

3.3.1. Start New Project

Now you will see the **Start Your New Project** screen:

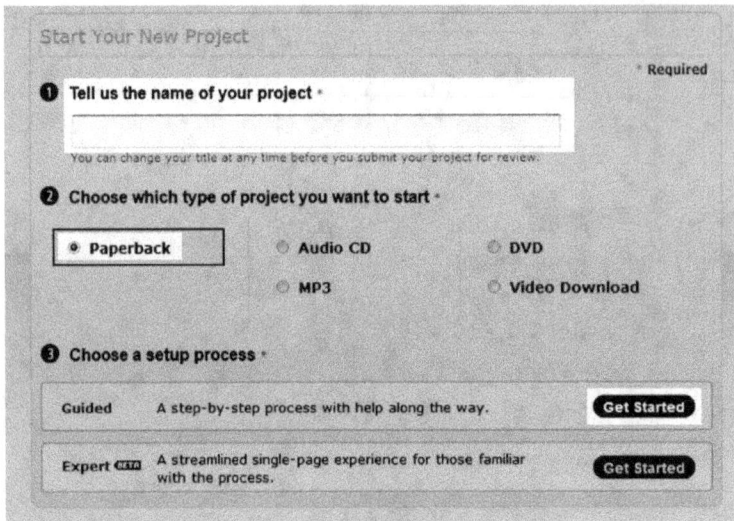

Figure 71 - Start New Project

You need to enter:

  - The **Name of Your Project**

  - The **type of project**

  - The **setup process** you wish to use:

    o **Guided**

    o **Expert**.

The first 2 steps of the setup process option are compulsory. For my book, I entered the initial details as follows:

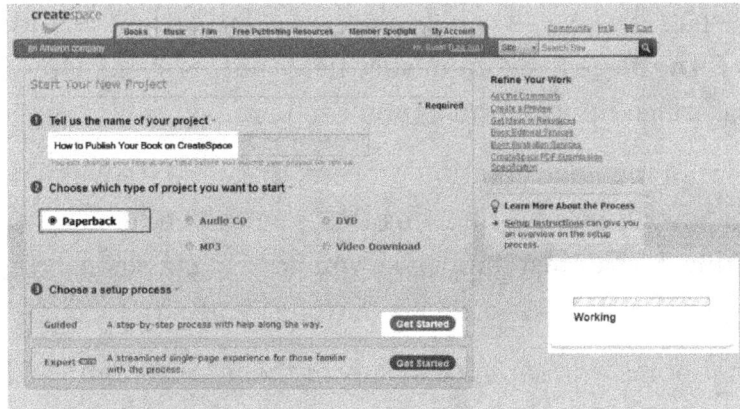

Figure 72 - Book Details Entered

- Once you've entered your book details correctly (if you make an error, don't worry, you can modify it afterwards), click on the **Get Started** button next to **Guided** (let's face it, if you can do **Expert,** you can skip this guide).

3.3.2. Title Information

Next, we enter the **Title Information:**

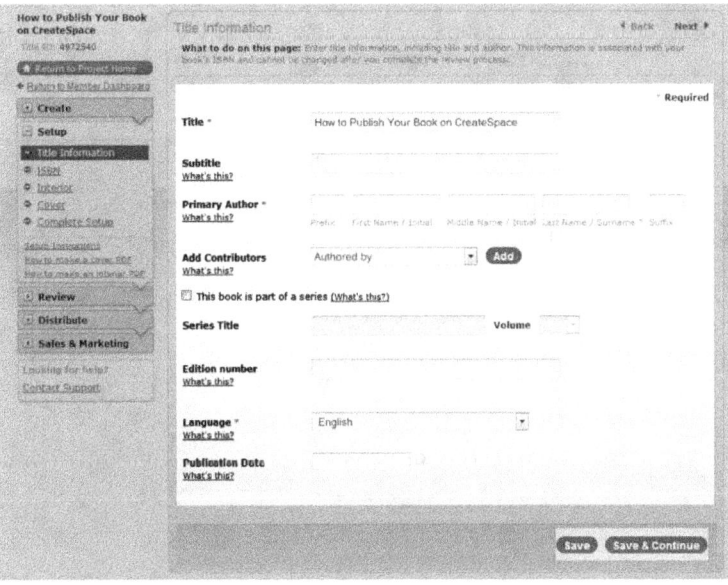

Figure 73 - Enter Title Information

Populate as much of this as you can, but only the **Title**, the **Primary Author,** and the book's **Language** are compulsory fields at this stage. However, it makes sense to enter as much information as you can here.

At a certain point in the book creation process, CreateSpace will tell you when the information becomes **locked**. Following this, you can't edit certain fields. Don't worry though, this doesn't just happen as you have to consciously agree to go past that particular point (you have to click a button saying so).

But, up until that point, you can modify any of the information you have entered; in fact, while writing this book, I changed both its title and subtitle.

3.3.2.1. *CreateSpace Help*

Also, under each of the field titles, there is a **What's This** popup hyperlink which you can click on to get help for that field. They're very useful:

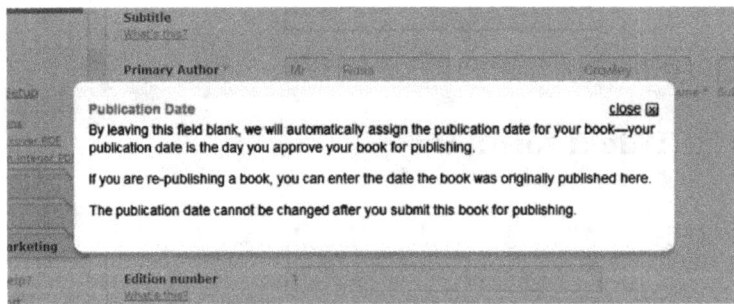

Figure 74 - What's This Help

1.   My title information is entered as follows:

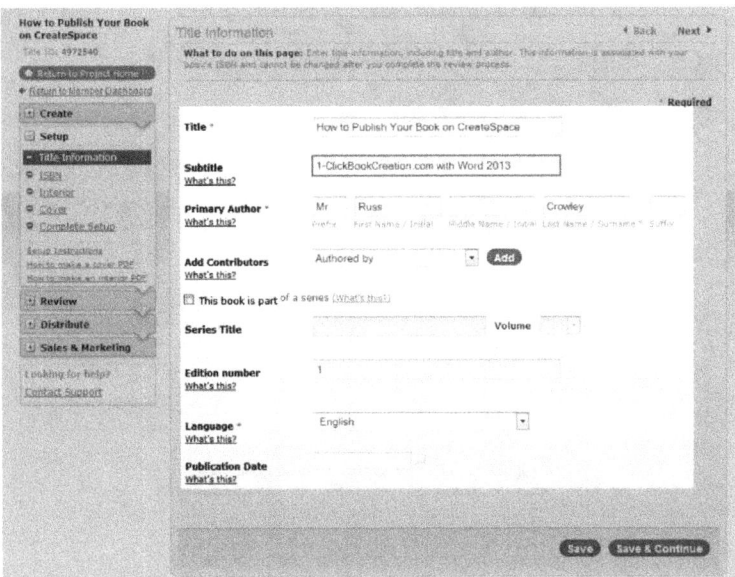

Figure 75 - Title Information Entered

2. If you want to save this information and stay on this page, click on **Save**. If you want to progress to the next step, click on **Save & Continue**.

   Once your information is saved, you can leave it, log-out, work on your book, come back after your scuba-diving holiday in the Maldives, whatever. It will still be there exactly how you left it the next time you login.

3.3.2.2. *Your Dashboard*

When you login, you will automatically be taken to your **dashboard** where you will see:

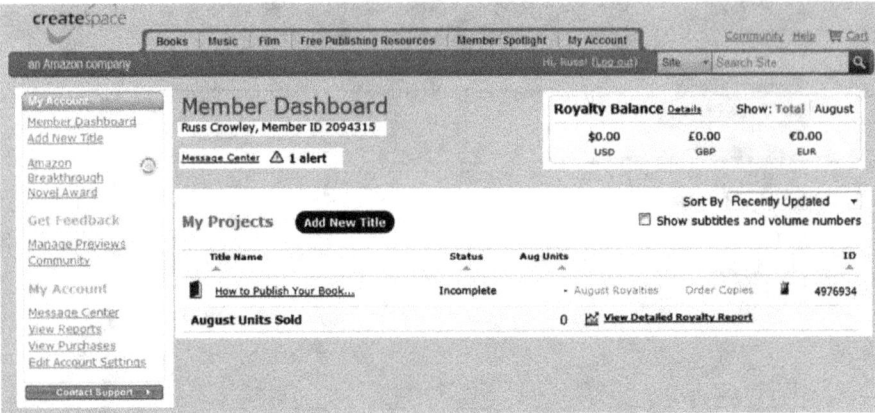

Figure 76 - Your Dashboard

Click on your book title to show your **Project** Homepage:

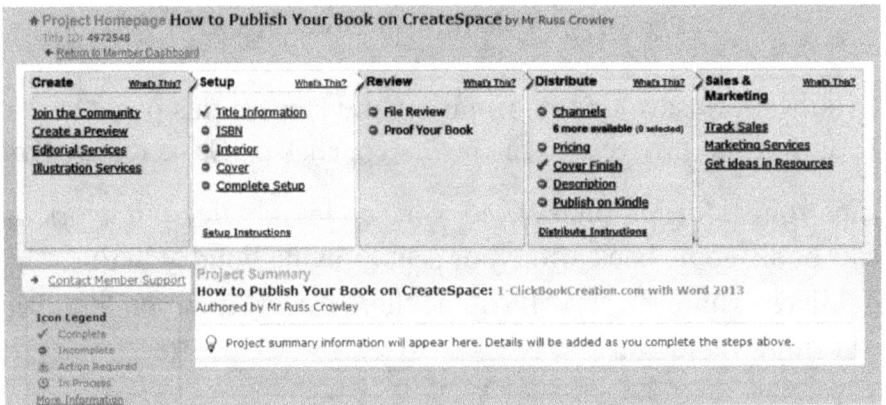

Figure 77 - Project Homepage

You can clearly see what areas are complete and what areas are not. In addition, though you can click on any of the links within a particular section, such as **Setup**, generally none of the links in the other sections will be available until the preceding section is complete.

Note: you will receive an alert soon after setting up your account (as shown in Figure 76—you can see it just below the Member ID), because CreateSpace requires you to enter your tax information. We will cover that in more detail in Appendix E.

3.3.3. ISBN

On the ISBN page, there are two options:

- Free CreateSpace-Assigned ISBN

- Provide Your Own ISBN:

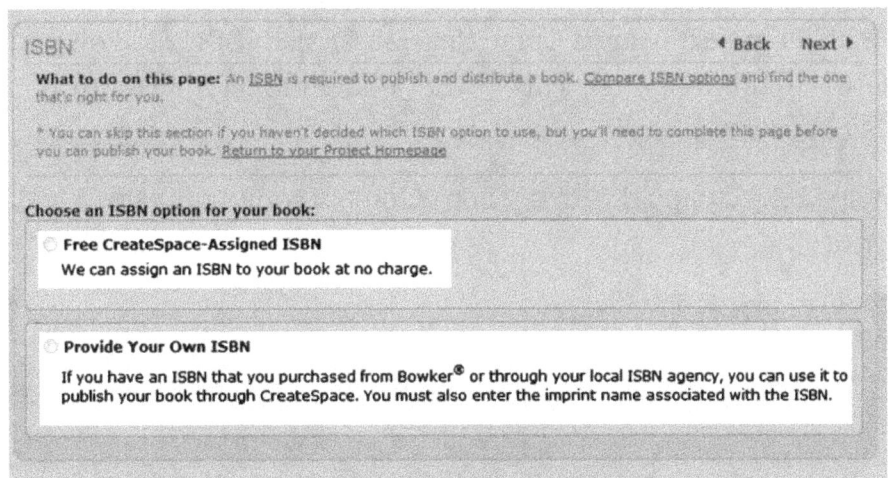

Figure 78 - ISBN Options

With Option 1, a **Free CreateSpace-Assigned ISBN**, you can assign an ISBN number to your book free-of-charge. Bear in mind that it's CreateSpace's ISBN number though, and you can only publish your book with them and on Amazon. Option 2 is where you assign your **own ISBN number**, or one that you obtained from a publisher, and you are then free to publish you book wherever you wish.

Note: once an ISBN number has been assigned to your book, it cannot be changed (though you can delete your entire project/title if you wish and start again).

Distribution Channels

CreateSpace currently has two main distribution channels: **standard distribution** and **extended distribution**; and these are further subdivided into six individual outlets (three in each). If you use your own ISBN number, only five of the six total outlets are available to you as, for some reason, you need to use a CreateSpace-assigned ISBN to make *Libraries and Academic Institutions* available.

> **Note:** if you have your own ISBN number, you can circumvent this by publishing your book with your own ISBN and then create an identical project using a CreateSpace-assigned ISBN to allow you access to this 6th outlet. This is what I have done for all of my books that have their own ISBN's.

> When I need to do this in my books, on my copyright page, I just write:

> *ISBN 978-1-908203-13-7*

> *ISBN 978-1496096951 (CreateSpace-assigned ISBN)*

> **Note:** don't forget, the barcode on your rear cover must match the actual ISBN number in use for that particular book though.

3.3.3.1. *CreateSpace-Assigned ISBN*

Though it is free, this option comes with the following conditions:

- CreateSpace Independent Publishing Platform is your book's imprint of record. If you select Amazon.com or Amazon's European websites as distribution channels, this imprint will be reflected on your book's detail page.

- You can sell your book through Amazon.com, Amazon's European websites, a CreateSpace eStore, and all Expanded Distribution channels (EDC).

- This ISBN can only be used with the CreateSpace Independent Publishing Platform.

- Your book's ISBN information will be registered with
  BooksInPrint.com®.

> *(The above is taken verbatim from CreateSpace:*
> *https://tsw.createspace.com/title/4972548/setup/book_isbn)*

Essentially, this means that you're locking your book into CreateSpace and to no other publishing platform. Of course, you retain full ownership of your book and all author rights relating to that book; and this also means that you can withdraw your book at any time should you wish to; but, just be aware of the above limitations.

3.3.3.2. Own ISBN's

Providing your own ISBN has greater advantages, but in many countries costs more. Naturally, you have none of the limitations from above and are free to publish your books wherever you wish, with the only restrictions being:

- If you are reprinting your book, the title, author name, and binding type must remain the same. A new edition requires a new ISBN.

- Your book's imprint must match what's on file with your ISBN.

> *(The above is taken verbatim from CreateSpace*
> *https://tsw.createspace.com/title/4972548/setup/book_isbn)*

These are standard restrictions anyway, so there aren't any real surprises.

For this book, I am going to select a **CreateSpace-assigned ISBN**.

1.   Click on **Assign Free ISBN**

     The screen refreshes, and my ISBN number has been assigned:

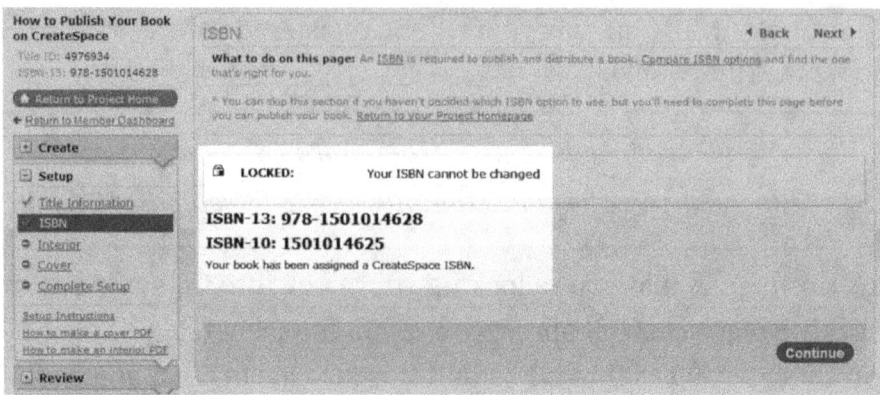

Figure 79 - ISBN Assigned

As Figure 79 shows, the ISBN is now locked to the book and cannot be changed. If you want to go back and create a new project using this book and then use your own ISBN, you can; but, for this project, the ISBN is locked. However, you can still modify all your title information at this stage.

2.   Click on **Continue** to start working on your **Interior**.

3.3.4. Interior

There are three settings to specify for the interior of your book: **Interior Type**, **Page Color**, and **Trim Size**. You need to select the options that you require before you proceed past this page and, more importantly, once your book's status is subsequently marked as **Available** (available for purchase), you will be unable to further modify the interior type or the trim size.

For further information on each item, refer to Appendix A.

- For **Interior Type**, you need to select either **Black & White** or **Full Color**. Apart from the look and feel of your book, the main effect of this will be the minimum list price for your book.

    As a rough guide, the minimum list price of color books costs 3-4 times as much as that of a black & white book.

    On this page, you can see a link which says, "**Estimate your book's manufacturing costs**." It's a good idea to click on this link to enable you to obtain an idea of the minimum pricing for your book.

I give an example in Appendix A.2, where this minimum list price of one of my color books practically forced me to publish a black & white version also. So it's worth bearing this in mind.

- For **paper type**, select either **white** or **cream**, depending on your own requirements.

- For **trim size**, this is the final size your book will be once it's printed, bound, etc. It is what you and your customers will physically hold, and it is worth noting that the trim size also affects the distribution options of your book, so refer to Appendix A.1 before you make your final decision.

  CreateSpace also gives you the options to download either a blank or a formatted Word template if you're unsure of how or where to start with your book.

Check out 1-ClickBookCreation.com for the quickest and easiest way to create your book in Word.

With full video training available, watch how to create your book with a single click and take it from the initial creation through to seeing it appear live on CreateSpace, Amazon, and KDP.

http://www.1clickbookcreation.com

You can come back and modify any of these settings all the way up to the point where your book becomes "**Available**."

Note: regardless of the trim size chosen, the cost per page is the same to the author, so a 5" x 8" page costs exactly the same as an 8.5" x 11" page.

For our *How to Read Thai* book, initially we wanted the trim size to be 6"x 9" to conform to the sizes of two of our other books: *Learning Thai, Your Great Adventure, and Learn Thai Alphabet with Memory Aids to Your Great Adventure*, but this would send the page count and the minimum price listing sky-high. As a result, we decided on an 8" x 10" trim size in the end.

3. For this book, I selected **Black & White** interior type, **8" x 10"** trim size, and **white** paper color.

At this point, you now have to upload your completed and finished manuscript to CreateSpace as a .pdf file.

You can probably see why it's important that you understand and know why you should select a particular trim size before you start formatting and laying out your document. If you don't, or you later decide to change it, then it's going to take you time to repaginate and reproof your book.

3.3.4.1. *CreateSpace Assistance*

Of course, assistance is available from CreateSpace should you wish to engage their services.

It's at this stage that, if you haven't done so already, you should turn your thoughts to your book covers (front, back, and spine), as once you've uploaded your interior file, you can proceed to work on your cover and upload it when complete.

3.3.5. *Cover*

Nothing draws customers more than a well-designed cover and I hope yours looks and says exactly what you want it to. If you don't have a cover yet, then you can use the CreateSpace **online cover creator**. Refer to Appendix B for further details.

The first choice you are faced with is to **Select a finish for your Book Cover**, and available options are either **Matte** or **Glossy**.

Like a lot of things, this comes down to personal preference, but make your selection:

1. Personally, I prefer a **Glossy** look to my books. I just think it looks better.

2. I'm not interested in the "Starting at $299" Professional Cover Design, so I will click on **Upload a Print-Ready PDF Cover**. You will see:

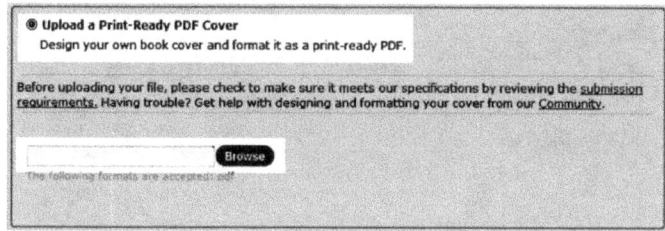

Figure 80 - Upload a Print-ready PDF Cover

As the instructions say, this needs to be a Print-ready PDF cover.

3. Click on **Browse**.

4. Navigate to and select your .pdf file.

5. Click **Ok** to upload it.

   The progress bar will display while your .pdf is uploading.

6. Once complete, you can click on **Save** to proceed to **complete setup**.

3.3.6. Complete Setup

To submit your book for the automated review—the first step in the CreateSpace review process—you need to upload both your interior file and your cover.

You don't have to do these at the same time, so if your cover is not ready, no matter, but you can't proceed past this point until both are complete, submitted, and approved.

The automated review process checks for things like embedded fonts, margins, ensuring printed text does not encroach into non-print areas, etc. The process for each is similar.

3.3.6.1. *Submitting Your Interior*

In addition to uploading and submitting your interior file, you also need to specify your book's attributes: the **Interior Type**, the **Paper Color**, and the **trim size**, as shown in Figure 81. Once you have done these, you can upload your interior file.

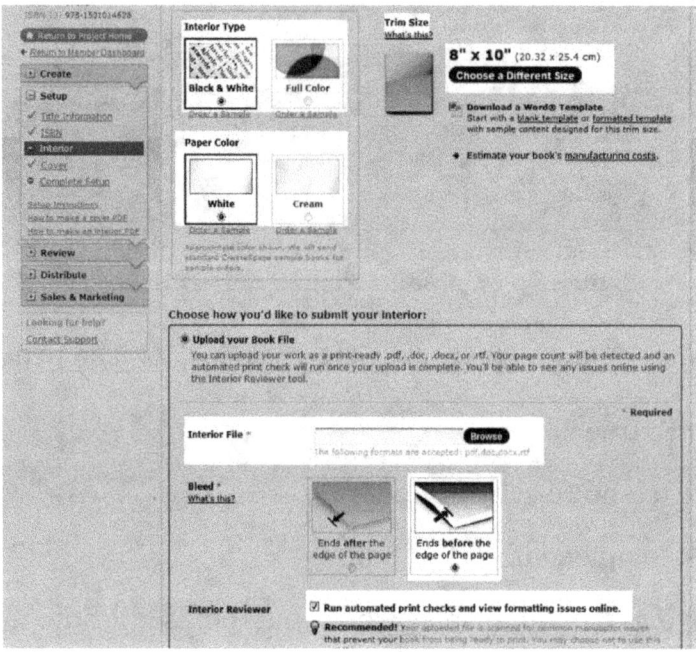

Figure 81 - Specify Interior Attributes

1. Click on the **Browse** button.

2. Navigate to and select your .pdf file to be uploaded.

3. Click **Okay**.

4. Select the **bleed** option for your book:

    – Ends **after** the edge of the page.

    – Ends **before** the edge of the page.

5. Ensure that the **Run automated print checks and view formatting issues online** option is selected.

6.   Click on **Save**, and your file will start to upload:

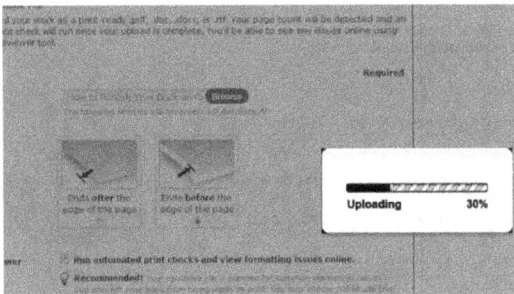

Figure 82 - Interior Uploading

Once your file has uploaded, CreateSpace will run the automated process to check your book for errors (if you did select that option, above):

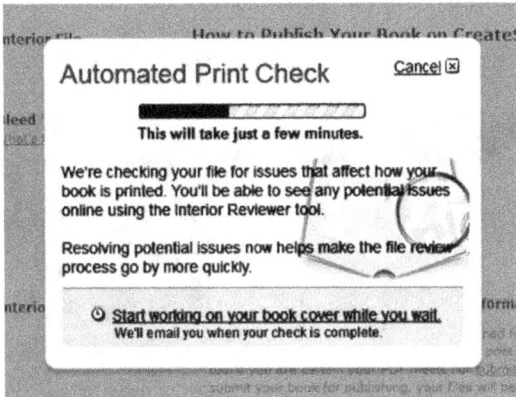

Figure 83 - Automated Print Check

If CreateSpace finds errors that will prevent your book from printing, you will need to resolve them before resubmitting; if any errors occur but do not prevent your book from being printed (and these do happen), you must manually select the option to ignore the errors and to continue the process past this point.

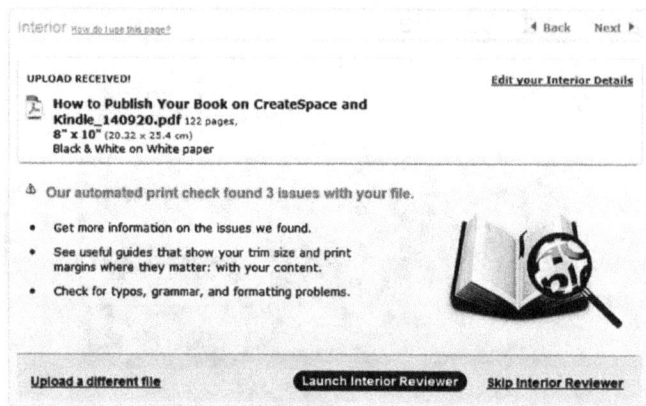

Figure 84 - Launch Interior Reviewer

For example, as Figure 84 shows, there are three mistakes with my submission, so I will review these. Please bear in mind that CreateSpace does make mistakes.

7. Click on **Launch Interior Reviewer**

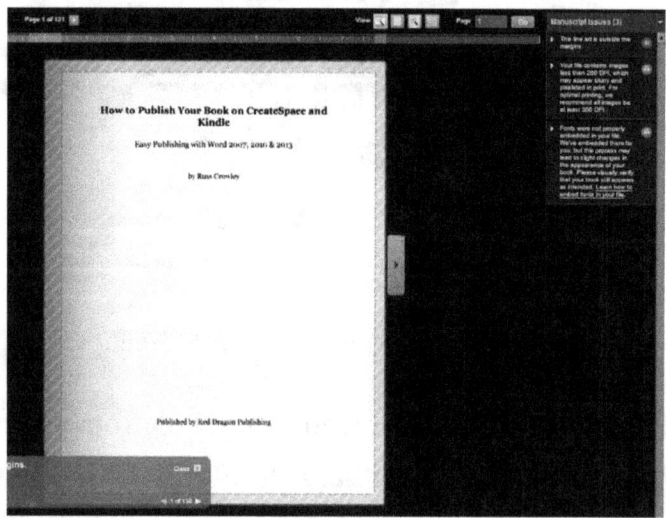

Figure 85 - Interior Review

8. Your errors will be listed on the page, and you can click to select and view each one. In Figure 85 CreateSpace has said, "This line art is outside the margins." I have no line art in the margins. Anywhere.

CreateSpace does get it wrong, so please be aware.

The other errors are inconsequential, so I can accept these and proceed with my cover.

9.   Click on **Ignore Issues and Save**.

10.   Then, back in the dashboard, click on **Ignore Issues and Continue**.

You can now submit your cover.

Note: the automated review process looks for formatting errors and items that are incorrect within your book; it does not proofread your text, it will not find spelling errors, it will not edit your document in any way—all of which needs to have been done before you reach this stage.

I cannot emphasize enough the importance of having another set of eyes looking over and reading your book in full.

Proofreading and editing can make such a difference to the success or failure of your book that it is inexcusable not to have someone else read it, preferably someone that has some skill, knowledge, and experience in this.

You may or may not be aware that bad reviews will kill your book. In itself, that's bad enough, but if the damning comments are as a result of poor formatting, layout, spelling errors, or what my old sport's teacher used to say, "*Schoolboy errors*," then you only have yourself to blame.

Please don't let it happen. There is no excuse.

We offer very reasonably priced proofing and editing services at www.russcrowley.com

But, if you seriously can't afford to pay to have it done, then refer to Appendix C for some best-practice suggestions.

3.3.6.2. *Submitting Your Cover*

There are only two steps here:

1. Select the finish for your cover: **matte** or **glossy**.

2. Then click on how you want to submit the cover of your book:

   – **Build your cover online** (refer to Appendix B).

   – **Professional Cover Design** (CreateSpace will help you here).

   – **Upload a Print-Ready PDF Cover**.

If you haven't already done this, for the latter option, click on it to select it, and then refer to section 3.3.5 of this book:

3.3.6.3. *Completing Setup*

You will now be shown the **Complete Setup** window which you can check and then submit your files for review:

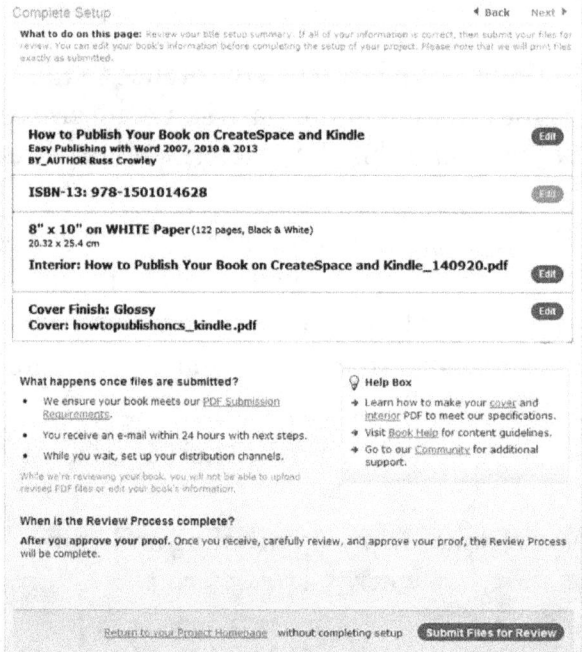

Figure 86 - Complete Setup

Once you have checked and verified this information (it should be straightforward, as all this has already been done), you can submit your files for manual review:

3.   Click on **Submit Files for Review**.

The screen will refresh and you will be told that your files are being checked. You can now setup your sales channels, etc. Refer to section 3.5.1.

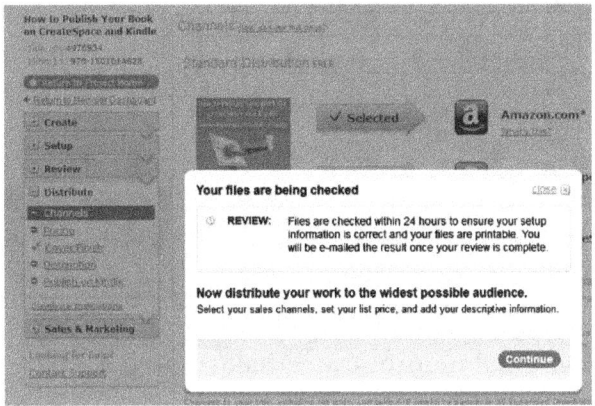

Figure 87 - Your Files Are Being Checked

The next step is the review process.

3.4.   Review

There are 2 steps listed in the dashboard, **file review** and **proof your book**.

3.4.1. File Review

This is all contained on the same page as the proofing (refer to Figure 86).

3.4.2. Proof Your Book

You will receive an email once the review of your book has completed. It will tell you whether your book can be approved or not:

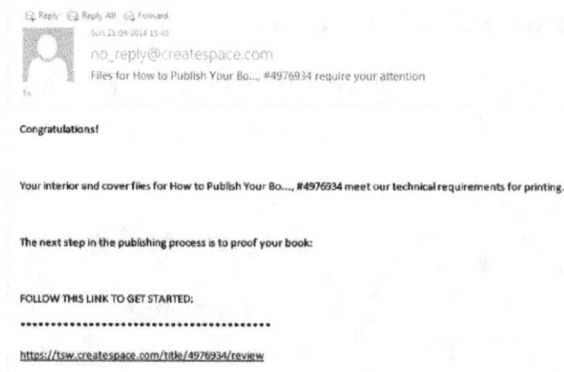

Figure 88 - Meet Requirements for Printing

You should now proof your book again. My advice is to always order a printed copy as reading it in its final medium will make a huge difference to what you see and read.

Either click on the link in the email, or login to your CreateSpace dashboard and go to the **Review** section.

You can either order a printed copy or you can view a digital proof (or both).

3.4.2.1. *Order a Printed Copy*

To order a printed copy:

1. Click on **Order a Printed Proof**

2. Then on the **Proceed to Cart** button.

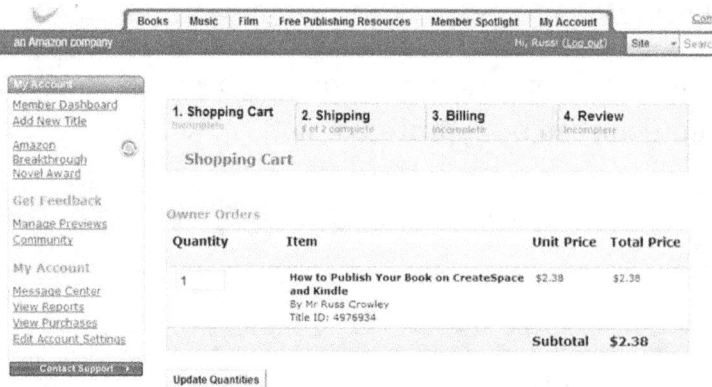

Figure 89 - Order a Printed Proof

3.   Follow the remainder of the process through to obtain your printed proof.
     This is self-explanatory.

3.4.2.2. *View a Digital Proof*

To view a digital proof:

1.   Click on **View a digital proof**

2.   Click on the **Launch Digital Proofer** button.

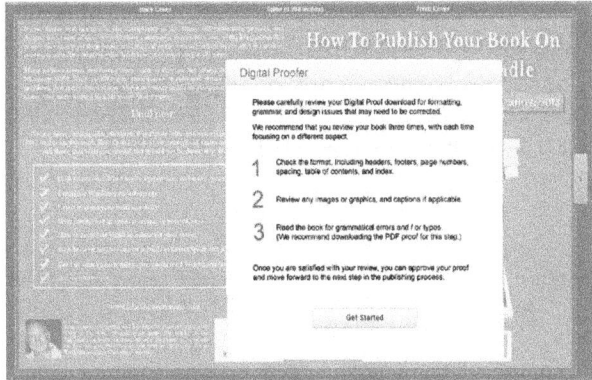

Figure 90 - Digital Proofer

Make sure that you read the instructions, in particular about how important it is
to do at least three passes on proofing your book, as shown in Figure 90. They
recommend:

1.   Check the format, including headers, footers, page numbers, spacing,
     table of contents, and index.

2.   Review any images or graphics, and captions if applicable.

3.   Read the book for grammatical errors and / or typos (We recommend
     downloading the PDF proof for this step).

It is advisable to download the .pdf and read it on your PC, or however you wish—
including printing it out if you can.

3.   Once you have completed your proof, you can click on the **Exit Digital
     Proofer** button.

You now have two options:

- Approve your book.

- Go back and make changes.

If you do the former, your book is ready to publish. If you do the latter, then you need to modify your interior and/or cover, and repeat the submission process again.

3.5. Distribute

Now that your book has passed the approval process, you can set your distribution channels, specify your book's pricing, your book description, and publish to Kindle. First, you need to set your channels:

3.5.1. Channels

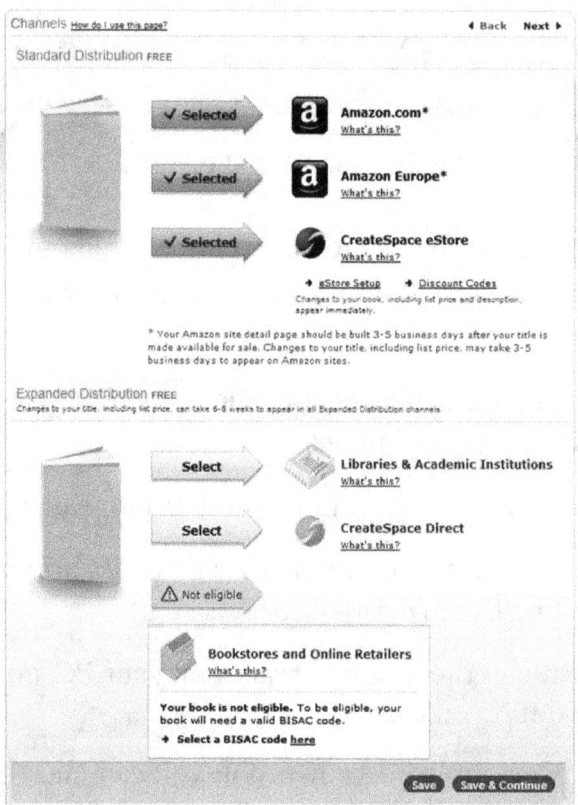

Figure 91 - Select Your Distribution Channels

As covered before in section 3.3.3, if you have selected to use a CreateSpace-assigned ISBN, then you have the option to select all six available channels; if you have used a non-CreateSpace-assigned ISBN, then not all options will be available to you.

As Figure 91 shows, all three **standard distribution** options are selected by default. It is up to you to select the **expanded distribution** options you require.

To add or remove a distribution outlet:

1. Click on the "**Select**" arrow. If selected, it will highlight blue, meaning that outlet is now available; if not selected, it will be grey.

    Note: you can also setup your CreateSpace **eStore** by clicking on that link, as well as setting up and applying discount codes (refer to Appendix D).

2. Once all options have been made, click on **Save & Continue**.

3.5.2. Pricing

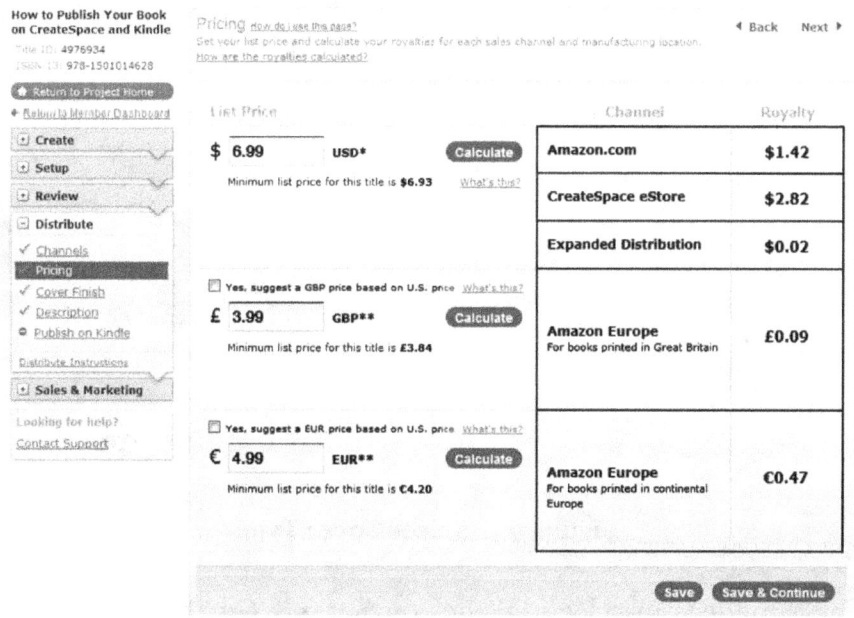

Figure 92 - Set Pricing Levels

Here you can set your book price across all your channels for the U.S.A., for Britain, and for Europe.

1.   Enter the price you wish to set for your book in the **List Price** field at the top.

2.   Click on **Calculate**. The royalty column will then populate with the earnings you will receive via the respective outlets for every sale of a book.

     If you have selected Britain and Europe, you have the options of clicking in the selection boxes to "**Suggest a figure based on the US price**." The table will recalculate each time.

3.   Click on **Save & Continue**.

3.5.3. *Cover Finish*

The cover finish is a straightforward choice between **matte** and **glossy** (and is a final repetition of this particular choice before your book goes live). Again, my own preference is glossy, but you can select the option you wish, and order a sample if you are unsure of the difference, or just prefer to.

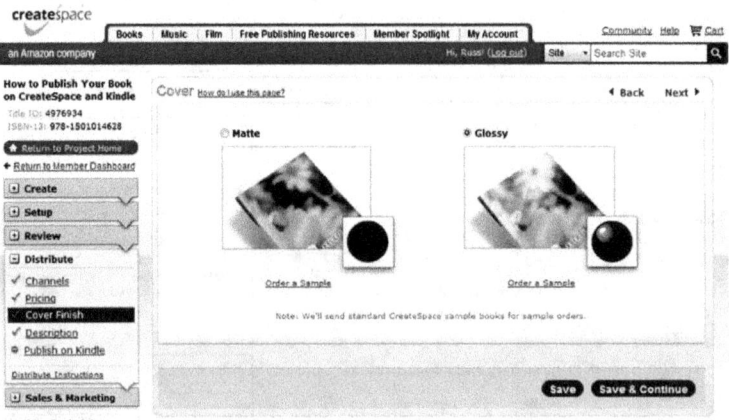

Figure 93 - Select Cover Type

Once you have made your selection, click on **Save & Continue.**

3.5.4. Description

The description is the collective term used for your book listing and sales channels and consists of: **description**, **BISAC category**, **author biography**, **book language**, **country of publication**, **search keywords**, and **large print**.

Only **Book Description** and **BISAC Category** are compulsory attributes, but as these attributes determine how and where your book is listed, it is important that you give these elements some thought.

> You've probably spent a lot of time preparing, writing, and formatting your book. Don't let it down by treating any of these description aspects as being any less important.

We'll look at them in the order that they appear on the web page, starting with your book description.

3.5.4.1. Description

The book description is a much-overlooked element by many people which, considering the time and effort that is put into writing the book, does seem rather strange.

Also, when you consider that you've probably spent a bit of time and money on creating a striking cover to draw a potential customer's eye, unless your goal is to **not** make sales, if you then let potential customers get away by telling them nothing of interest, or presenting a total lack of information about what your book is about and what it can do for them, it must make you wonder why you actually wrote the book in the first place?

Your keywords and title will help people find you; your book cover and title will bring them to your page; the *look-inside* feature will give them a brief taste; but, with an undecided viewer, it's likely that your book description will tip the balance in your favor, so make it count.

As this is a crucial component—remember, your budding buyer will probably read this long before they get your book—its importance cannot be understated; and, to let you wrap your book's tentacles around them, to suck them in, and make it impossible to leave without buying, CreateSpace gives you 4,000 characters for this. This works out to approximately 750 words if you also include HTML tags, so I would recommend that you use it wisely.

So, what do you write?

Your USP

Tell the reader what your **USP**, your **Unique Selling Point**, is. Why this book, why you (as the author)? No one else is going to shout about why they need your book, and unless you tell them why the biggest mistake in their life would be to leave your Amazon book page without a purchase, they might. Treat it like it's the last time you will ever see them again (if you know what I mean?), like it's the only chance you have got of convincing them to click on the buy button.

This is essential, purely because it probably is the one and only chance you're going to get. There are hundreds, maybe even thousands of books being published each day, and if you don't convince the reader of your value now, if you can't convince them to buy, then there is zero guarantee that they will ever come back.

Make your description count.

You have 4,000 characters, so use them.

Don't even think about **not** using HTML, it's really simple[5]. If you don't use HTML tags to stand out from the rest, then your text will just look like a...well, a

---

[5] Some authors and books will tell you it doesn't matter about HTML tags or not, plain text will do; that's up to them, but if used correctly, then it may draw attention to those aspects that you are trying to promote and may make the difference between a sale and no sale. It's up to you of course, but I would recommend it. You can always tweak it and see what works best.

block of text; however, if you use HTML tags, then it becomes a powerful sales tool; and, it could be the difference between the top 100 and the top 100,000.

Also important is the category of your book.

3.5.4.2. *BISAC Category*

The Book Industry Standards and Communications (BISAC) category is used by the book-selling industry to group books to aid identification and searching.

1. Click on **Choose**, and the following will display:

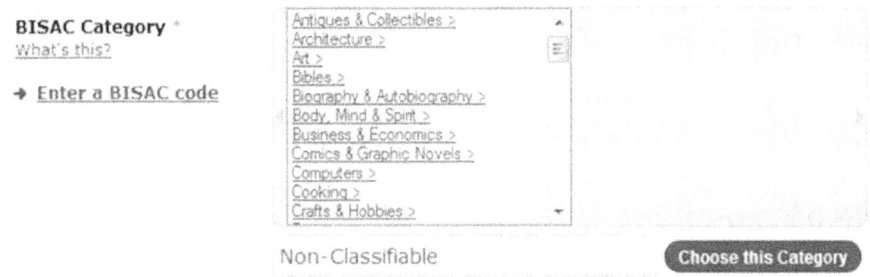

Figure 94 - BISAC Category

2. Navigate through the list and select first the category that you want, and then the sub-category.

    Once you have identified the correct category for your book, click on **Choose this Category**.

Note: if you already know your BISAC code, as opposed to searching for it, you can click on **Enter a BISAC code** and then enter it in the field.

If you wish to look at the complete list of BISAC codes, then you can go to: https://www.bisg.org/complete-bisac-subject-headings-2013-edition

Now we'll look at the optional fields in this section.

3.5.4.3. *Author Biography*

This is where you can tell your potential buyers a little bit about yourself; or, actually, as CreateSpace allows you to use 2,500 characters here (according to them, that's about 470 words), you can tell them quite a lot.

Use this section to tell the reader about your background, any qualifications, expertise, other works, why you wrote this book, and any personal interests that relate to *this subject*.

Ultimately, your entire description should be about positioning yourself and trying to create a bond between you and your reader; and, if you can establish a level of trust, albeit small, then your battle is almost over. Therefore, if you can interweave your book description and your bio into a single, solid message that resonates with your audience, then I'm sure your book sales will reflect this.

3.5.4.4. *Book Language*

The book language is a straightforward drop-down list, so select the appropriate language from those available. I'm very pleased to see the list contains "**English**," and not *American English*, or *International English*.

3.5.4.5. *Country of Publication*

Your country of publication needs to be either the U.S.A., or the country which is associated with your ISBN numbers. So, if you selected a CreateSpace-assigned ISBN number, you need to select **United States** from the drop-down list.

3.5.4.6. *Search Keywords*

CreateSpace allows you to add five-keywords or "keyword phrases," each of which should be separated by commas. Ensure that you use all five, and they are relevant to your book and the niche or category your book is in.

My recommendation is to spend some time searching for similar books in the niche or the genre your book relates to, and then identify the main keywords that the top 10, 20, or even 30 books in your niche use, and use them.

Remember, your book is always here on CreateSpace and you can modify your keywords anytime you like. Amazon is also faster at replicating information, as only a few years ago a 1-3 days wait meant exactly that, but now, in my experience, book changes tend to appear within 24-hours.

Tweak and re-tweak, it's worth it.

3.5.4.7. *Contains Adult Content*

If your book's details page contains material which is unsuitable for minors (<18 years of age), then you need to select this option. This means that your book will not show up, or show inappropriate content where it shouldn't. According to CreateSpace's "**what's this**" link, no modifications will be made to the information entered.

3.5.4.8. *Large Print*

If your book's audience is sight-impaired and your font is sized 16-points or over, then select this box to ensure that your book's product detail age will be marked "large print" in the Amazon search results.

Selecting this option doesn't mean your book is limited to just the large print listings, it will appear in other results also.

Once all your details are correct, either click on **Save** or **Save & Continue** to go to "Publish on Kindle."

3.6.   **Publishing on Kindle**

CreateSpace offer a "publish to Kindle" process, but we cover that in more detail in sections 4 and 5.

Next is CreateSpace's sales and marketing services.

3.7.   **Sales & Marketing**

CreateSpace offer a number of professional services to promote and market your book, including: editing, layout and design, Kindle, and marketing. All the figures listed below, and the summary of information are taken from the CreateSpace website and are correct at the time of writing; but, it is your responsibility to check and verify all prices and services offered.

- **Editing services** include (price is for first 10,000 words, additional costs thereafter):

    – Single-pass editing:

        o **Copyediting** ($160) – a single-pass encompassing grammar, punctuation, and spelling

        o **Line-editing** ($210) – a single-pass encompassing structure, plot flow, characterisation, tone, grammar, punctuation, and spelling.

    – Multi-round Editing

        o **Editing Package** ($300) – 2 rounds of editing: 1 on structure, plot flow, characterisation, and tone; and the other on grammar, punctuation, and spelling.

        o **Editing Package** plus ($470) – 3 rounds of editing: 2 passes on structure, plot flow, characterisation, and tone; and, grammar, punctuation, and spelling for the 3rd.

- **Layout & Design**, including:

    – Interior Options:

        o **Supported PDF Interior** ($140) – this takes your preformatted file and readies it for publishing.

        o **Simple Interior** ($199) – this takes your ready file and inserts it into 1 of 10 preformatted templates.

        o **Simple Custom Interior** ($349) – if your manuscript does not have complex formatting and has either one image or none, then you could use this option.

        o **Moderate Custom Interior** ($579) – if your layout is even more complex than will fit into those options above, then this should do it for you.

    – Cover:

- o **Supported Cover** PDF ($99) — this is where you've designed your own cover, but need some assistance.

- o **Custom Cover** ($399) — KDP will create a custom cover with one image, custom layout, colors and typography.

- o **Custom Cover Premier** ($599) — their premier package (I guess you get it all).

- **Kindle**:

  - **Kindle Conversion** ($79) — this appears to be a straightforward re-pagination and formatting service from .pdf to Kindle.

  - **Complex Kindle Conversion** ($139) — if your book has more complex formatting, then you'll need to pay a little more.

  - **Children's Conversion** ($149) — the description also references complex formatting, but I'm unclear why this complex formatting is more complex than the $10-cheaper complex formatting (above).

- **Marketing Services** include:

  - **Marketing Copy Essentials** ($249) — which includes, among others: a one-line marketing pitch for your book (a tagline); a BISAC category; five keywords; book description, 200 words maximum; author biography (any of these sound familiar?) and they will also provide back cover text for your book.

  - **Kindus Review** ($425, standard; $575, express) — *Kindus* are a leading publishing industry voice and a positive review from them will surely help your sales.

  - **Library of Congress Assignment** ($25) — a unique *Library of Congress Control Number* (LCCN) is assigned to your book to catalog and other processing activities, such as making it easier for other databases to link to and find your book

RUSS CROWLEY PUBLISHING

So, as you can see, though CreateSpace wants to help you publish your book with them, they don't offer much beyond the very basic help for free; for the rest, you need to engage their services.

In contrast, I can provide you with cost-effective publishing services and more at www.russcrowley.com.

If you're interested, check us out:

4. Formatting for Kindle

Once you've uploaded your printed book to CreateSpace, the next step is they will ask you to send it across to Kindle; and, from what they say, all you need to do is login, populate a few detail fields, and click "publish"...and...and...Whoooosh, your book is now on Kindle...

Guess what?

It doesn't quite work like that.

Yes, you can do that, but it'll probably look terrible.

Why?

Well, Kindle has strict guidelines on what will and won't work for formatting books and then publishing to their platform.

In CreateSpace, on the **Publish on Kindle** page, scroll to the bottom of the page and click on "**How do I publish on Kindle**."

You'll find a line which reads:

> *However, file conversion can produce varied results. For best results, KDP recommends that you upload your content in either Microsoft Word or HTML format.*

> *(https://www.createspace.com/Help/Index.jsp?orgId=00D300000*
> *001Sh9&id=50170000000jXyB)*

The problem here is that CreateSpace wants to send your book across as a .pdf, which is neither of those recommended options.

Yes, I realize that if you followed this guide through, then your book originated in Word, but submitting as a PDF isn't ideal.

The question is, do you trust it?

If you want to ask me if I trust it, then the answer has to be a resounding **no,** not a chance.

Furthermore, if after you've created your Kindle account and you're setting up your title, if you try and upload a .pdf, this is what you'll see:

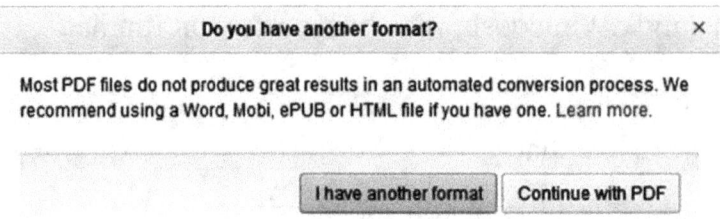

Figure 95 - Kindle: Do You Have Another Format

So, straight-away we have a conflict here: CreateSpace is telling you it is okay, but Kindle is saying otherwise.

Ultimately, formatting needs to be platform-specific and, if you've gone to all the trouble of writing and creating your masterpiece, why would you risk letting it all go at this stage. So, what do you do next?

4.1.   The Next Step?

Well, the best thing to do is to take your original manuscript/book and reformat it for Kindle.

My own personal recommendation is to **never use** the CreateSpace *send-to-Kindle* function, it's just too hit-and-miss; and, at the very least, there is a free Kindle formatting guide available on the Kindle website that you can follow and use to reformat your original manuscript.

Of course, that is just one option. Another is to get someone else to do it. However, believe me, though it isn't particularly difficult to do yourself, the time it takes will depend on your skill with Word and the size and complexity of your book.

If your book is large but has a simple layout, then it is really easy. If it's got a complex layout, then that might be a little difficult; but, you can work out how to do it yourself. It's all about formatting and what works and what doesn't work. The problem is, it can be time-consuming.

If you have the fully licensed version of the **1-Click Book Creation** template, then it's as easy as clicking on a button; but, if you don't, then please follow the instructions below.

The first step is to either create a new book or, as we've already written this one, to **Save As** and mark it Kindle in some way, so you can identify it. Then, we just need to setup our book. Before we do that though, I'll identify some fundamental differences:

- Kindle does not use headers and footers, or page numbers, so we need to get rid of all of them.

- If you didn't insert your pictures as shown in section 2.10, then you'll have to go back and do them all again (it's a pain, but you have to do it this way).

- If you've used **drop capitals**, remove them.

- You will need to remove all bullet lists from your document as, though bullets can be used in Kindle documents, the code uses a different format and can't read the ones that Word uses directly.

- Remove any footnotes.

- Remove all page breaks. Kindle will repaginate based on the **Heading 1 settings** which, in my template, are already configured with an automatic page break before.

- Remove all tab characters.

- Remove optional and non-breaking hyphens.

- Remove manual line breaks.

- Remove borders, columns, text wrapping (refer to inserting pictures again, if necessary), text boxes, Word Art, etc.

As far as I'm aware, that's pretty much it for what you can and can't do. If you implement them, then it'll look much better and the submission process to KDP will be much smoother.

4.2.   Page Setup

As we did in section 2.2.1, go to **Page Layout > Size > More Paper Sizes** and set your page size to **6 x 8 inches** (6 inches wide, 8 inches tall). This is the Kindle page size and is chosen purely to give you an indication of how your book will probably look on the Kindle (note the word 'probably'). If your original trim size was smaller than this, reformatting should be simple. If it was larger, it will require a little more work.

Note: the best way to submit to Kindle from Word is actually via Web-filtered HTML, but setting up the page in this manner will give you an approximate look and feel for your finished product (please note the word "approximate").

- Ensure **Apply to** is set to **Whole Document**. It's quite possible (and usual) for Word to ignore this and just apply it to the section, so:

- Turn on the **Navigation Pane (View > Navigation pane)**, then click on **Pages** to view your book as thumbnail images. Then you can quickly scroll through to ensure that all sections have resized correctly. If they haven't, repeat the resize process (above) for each incorrectly sized section.

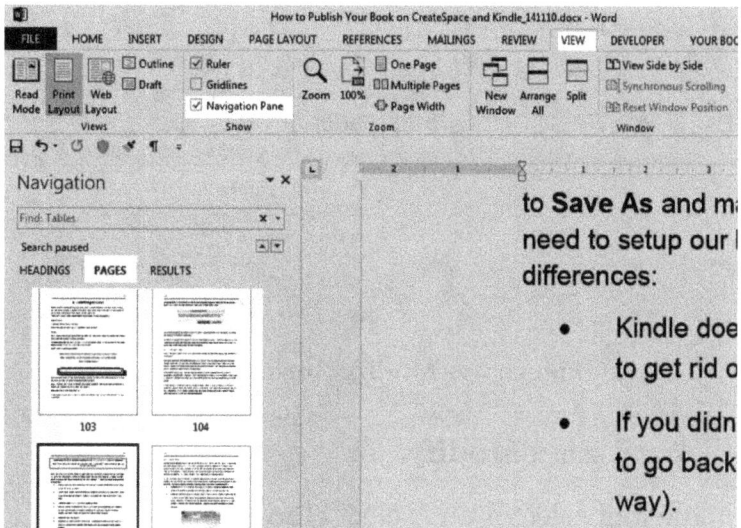

Figure 96 - Quickly View Trim Sizes

4.3.   Set Margins

Set your left and right page margins to 0.75", and your top and bottom margins to 1".

If you had to go through and change the page sizes of individual sections in the previous steps, you will probably have to repeat this for the margins in each section.

4.4.   Change the Default Font

Arial or other non-serif fonts don't work too well on a Kindle as they're considered difficult to read; and, on the newer Kindles, the default font is Georgia; that's what I prefer to use.

To change the default font in your book:

1.   Click on **Home** on the menu bar.

2.   In the styles ribbon, find **Normal**:

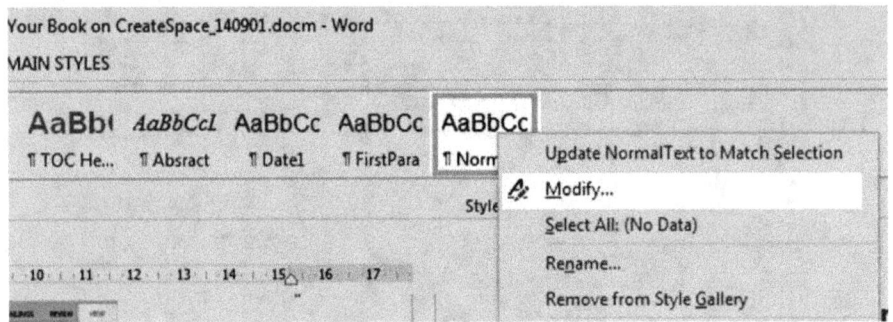

Figure 97 - Modify Normal Style

3.   Right-click and select **Modify.**

4.   Click on the font selector and select **Georgia.**

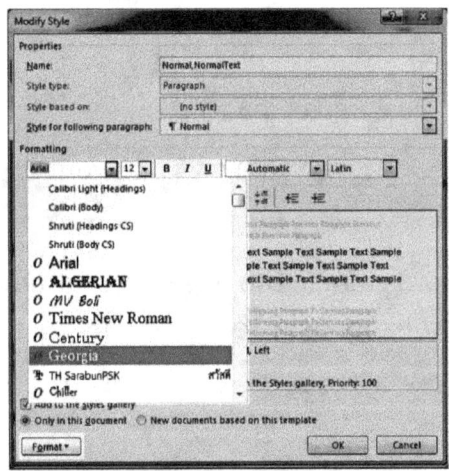

Figure 98 - Change Font

5.   Also, while we're here, we'll change some other settings. Click on **Format**, in the bottom left of the dialog box.

6.   Select **Paragraph** and set **Spacing before** to 0 points; and **spacing after** to 12 points. Set **line spacing** to **Single**:

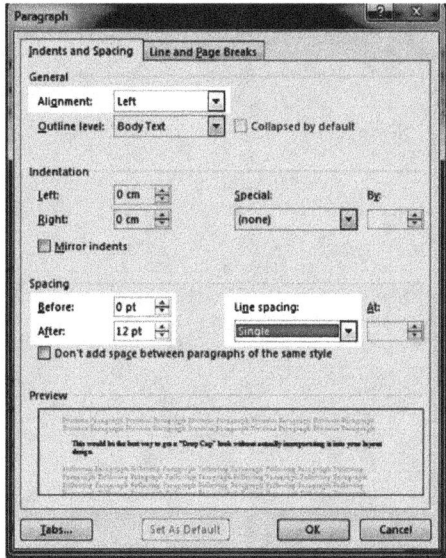

Figure 99 - Normal Style Paragraph Options

7.   Click **Ok**. This will change the default style to **Georgia**.

You will notice in Figure 99 (or in the style itself), that the alignment is set to **Left**. This is how I like my text, I'm not a big fan of **Justified**; however, this is my preference, if yours is otherwise, then you can set the alignment that way.

4.5.   Change Styles

This might seem like a lot to do, but trust me, once you've done it once, the rest is simple.

You need to verify and perhaps change your heading styles, it all depends on how you've set your template up. The following lists the sizes and attributes that I use myself. You can change these in exactly the same way as in section 4.4:

- Heading 1
    - Size—16 pts
    - Space before—0
    - Space after—24
- Heading 2

- – Size—14 pts
- – Space before—0
- – Space after—12
- Heading 3
  - – Size—12
  - – Space before—0
  - – Space after—12
- Heading 4
  - – Size—12
  - – Space before—0
  - – Space after—12
- Paragraph (Body, ParaIndent, and all Indent styles)
  - – Size—12
  - – Space before—0
  - – Space after—12
- Title
  - – Size—16
  - – Space before—24
  - – Space after—24
- Subtitle
  - – Size—13
  - – Space before—0
  - – Space after—12

Once you have modified these, your book should look great.

4.6.   Tables

The Kindle doesn't like tables and the best way to handle these is to take a snapshot/image of the table and then insert it into Kindle as a picture. It's not great, but these are the limitations. The way I do it is to:

1. Press the Print Screen button on my keyboard (**prt scr**).

2. I use Photoshop, so the following is applicable to that. If you use something different, then a similar process will be available in your particular app.

3. Create **New (Ctrl+N)**.

4. Paste my screenshot in (**Ctrl+V**).

5. Crop and modify as required.

6. **Save** the image.

7. Insert the picture using Word's **Insert Picture** functionality.

8. Right-click on the image and select **Insert Caption**

9. Don't forget to change the label to **Table**.

10. Update your **Table of Tables** (if you have one).

4.7.   Pictures

As mentioned before, ensure that you use Word's built-in **Insert Picture** functionality to place your pictures. Otherwise your pictures might not display (it will look terrible on the Kindle).

You don't have to downscale your 300 dpi images, as saving the Word document as **Web-filtered HTML** will do this for you (refer to section 4.9.1).

4.7.1. Duplicate Pictures

Once you have inserted an image correctly using the **Insert > Pictures** process, you can then copy and paste duplicate images within that document: Word will insert the duplicate image as a link, saving file size.

Note: never apply a border to any picture in Word, as this could affect the scaling and resizing of the image.

4.8. Bookmarks

As part of its navigation and setup, Kindle requires that your book has at least two bookmarks: bookmarks are navigation points in your document—**start** and **toc**. **Start** marks the first page of your content, and **toc** marks where your ToC is. If your book doesn't have these, you need to insert them.

1. Go to the ToC heading in your book (the actual heading entitled "Table of Contents" itself).

2. Put your cursor at the beginning of the word "Table."

3. Click on **Insert > Bookmark**.

4. Enter **toc** (all lowercase) in the bookmark dialog:

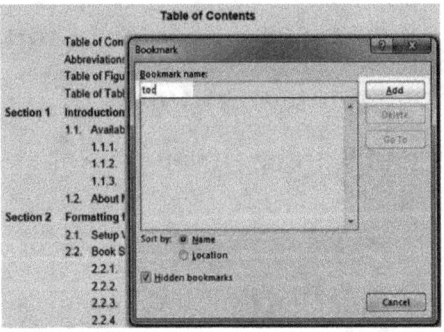

Figure 100 - Insert Bookmark (toc)

5. Click on **Add.**

6. Go to Section 1 (or to the start of the very first chapter of your book).

7. Click on **Insert > Bookmark**.

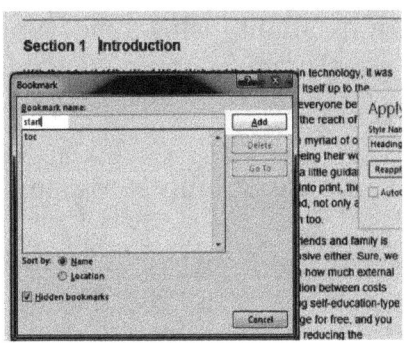

Figure 101 - Insert Bookmark (start)

8.   Type in **start**.

9.   Click on the **Add** button.

The two bookmarks required by Kindle have now been added.

4.9.   Export to HTML

Once you've finished authoring your book, you need to export it to HTML, as though Kindle does accept Word documents, in the same way as I wouldn't send a .pdf across, neither would I submit a Word document.

Yes, it may work, but at the moment it's not too great a process and is hit-or-miss if you go beyond the basics. If you use HTML, then you can get a better idea of what you're sending across and what the end result will look like. Yes, Word's HTML output isn't great, but technology has improved and the Kindle converter has apparently been optimised for Word HTML.

1.   The first thing that you should do is save your document. Don't lose any unsaved errors.

2.   Then, click on **File** > **Save As**.

3.   Select the File Location.

4.   From the **Type** drop-down menu, select **Web Page, Filtered**.

5.   Here, in terms of file size, you're trying to save the file with as small a file size as possible.

If you receive a warning about losing formatting, you can ignore it (remember, we saved the file in step 1, so we're only working on a copy anyway).

6.   You may also receive a compatibility message:

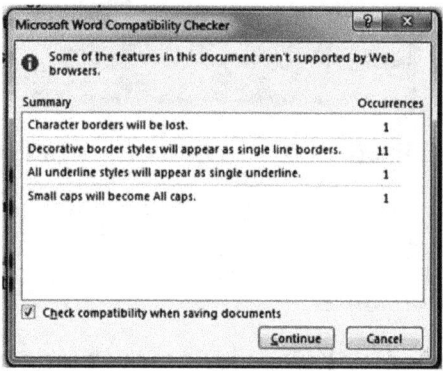

Figure 102 - HTML Compatibility Checker

7.   Either cancel and go back and address these issues, or click on **Continue.**

8.   If you are using the **1-Click Book Creation template**, you will receive a message about losing macros:

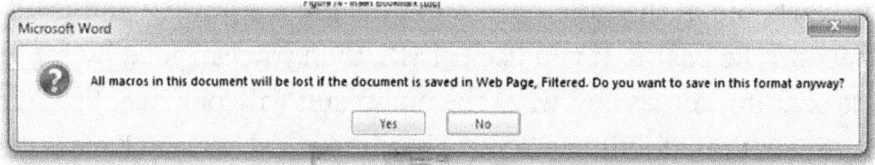

Figure 103 - Losing Macros

9.   Click on **Yes**.

10.   Your document will now save and display as filtered HTML.

4.9.1. *Exported Pictures*

If your book contains images, Word will have exported them all to a separate folder in the same directory as you saved the book:

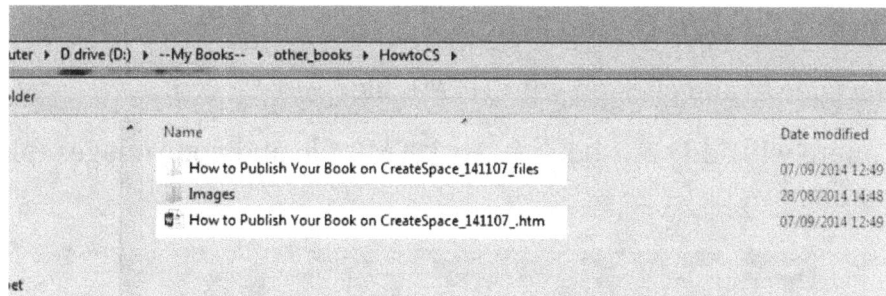

Figure 104 - Saved Image Files

Do not modify the file names or move images into or out of this folder. The HTML document has links to each image and if you modify the names, it won't be able to find them.

With that in mind, we can now convert the HTML file to the format for Kindle, and for this you need a free program called *Calibre*.

4.10.   Calibre

Calibre is an ebook management tool that is excellent for converting HTML to mobi format (that required by Kindle).

1.   Download Calibre: from http://calibre-ebook.com/download

2.   Install it and open it.

Figure 105 – Calibre

3. Click on the **Add Books** button.

4. Navigate to and click on your HTML file.

5. Calibre will add your book (your HTML file and your images folder) as a zip file:

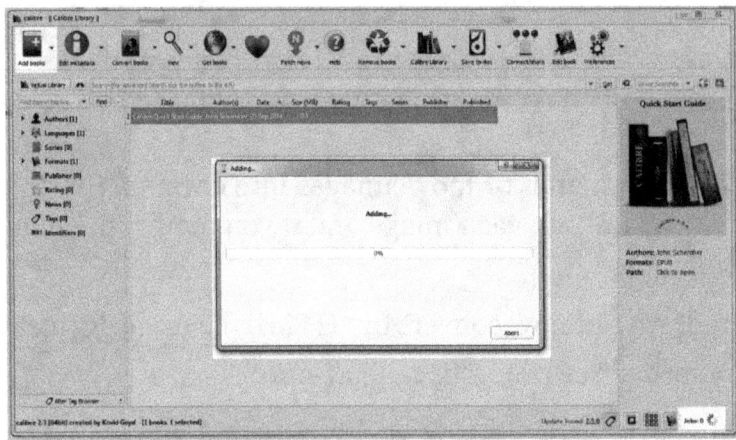

Figure 106 - Adding Your HTML File

If you want to, you can use Calibre as an ebook library tool, click on the **metadata** button, enter your book's details, and upload your cover file, etc., but we're just concerned with exporting to Kindle here, so:

6. Click on **Convert Books**

Now, I am not a Calibre expert so I go with the default settings and it works just fine.

7. If you want to specify a particular device to format it for (and to preview it in), then click on the **Page Setup** tab, and select your required Kindle device:

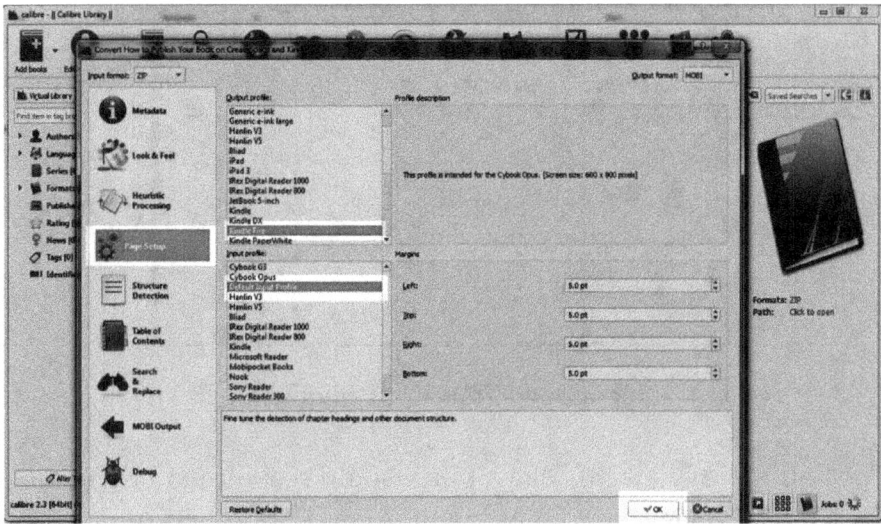

Figure 107 - Page Setup

8.   Other than that, we're good to go. Click on **Ok**.

The conversion process will take place:

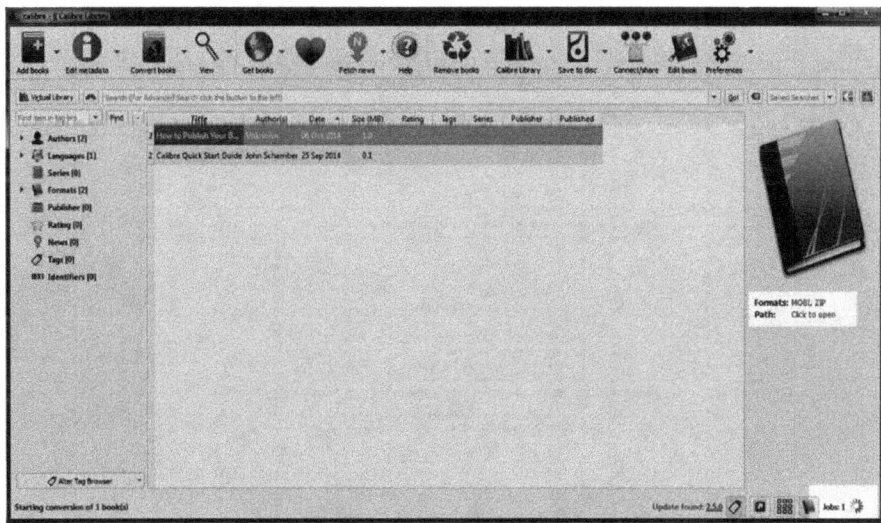

Figure 108 - MOBI Conversion

9.   Once complete, click where it says "**mobi**" to open the converted file:

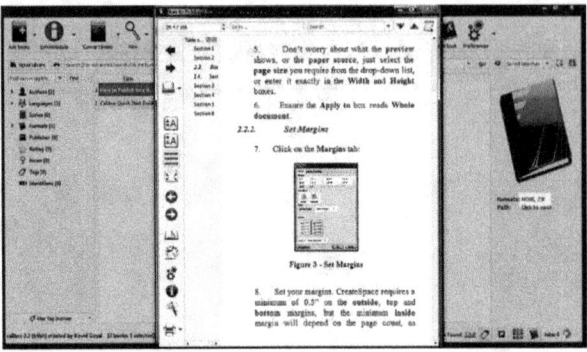

Figure 109 - Calibre Previewer

10. The Calibre previewer is okay, but I would recommend that you download the Kindle Previewer from Amazon.

     The link is long and complicated, so I would suggest going to your preferred search engine and searching for **Kindle Previewer**.

Installing this and viewing your mobi file in the previewer is straightforward, but I must emphasize the importance of doing this as, other than opening it on an actual Kindle, this is the best way to see how your finished book will look.

Figure 110 - Kindle Previewer

You should go through the entire book to ensure that it looks how you want it.

If you need to change anything, then you will either need to go back to your original Word document, the one you marked as the Kindle version, or the version you used for your CreateSpace version, and make the changes there. Then, you will need to export to HTML again.

Alternatively, if it is just a look-and-feel issue, then you can get away with just modifying the HTML file. However, modifying HTML is outside the scope of this book. Again, go to your favorite search engine and search for tutorials on modifying HTML and Cascading Style Sheets (CSS).

5. Publishing to Kindle

If you've skipped the other sections to come straight here, though CreateSpace offers an easy-to-use facility to publish your book to Kindle, I wouldn't recommend it. It's simple to do manually, and that's what I would suggest as you then retain full control over the process.

5.1. Create a Kindle Account

1. Go to http://kdp.amazon.com and click on **Sign-up.**

2. Enter your email address and select **I am a new customer**.

3. Enter your **name.**

4. Enter your **password** (and again to confirm).

5. Click on **Create Account**.

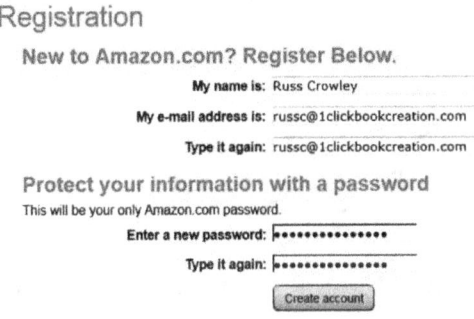

Figure 111 - Register for Kindle

6.   You will receive a message saying that your account is incomplete. Follow the information given to complete this.

7.   Next, you will be directed to your account profile, where you will need to update your company/publisher, your tax information, and your payment information.

That's it, you're done.

5.2.   Complete Your Account Information

Once you're logged-in, you will need to complete your account information to be able to publish your book.

1.   Click on **Update Now**

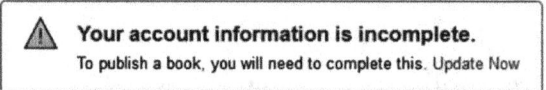

Figure 112 - Update Account Information

The next step requires you to provide your **company information**, **tax information**, your **bank account details** for royalty payments, and to select the **marketplaces** you wish your book to appear in:

2.   Enter your company/publisher information:

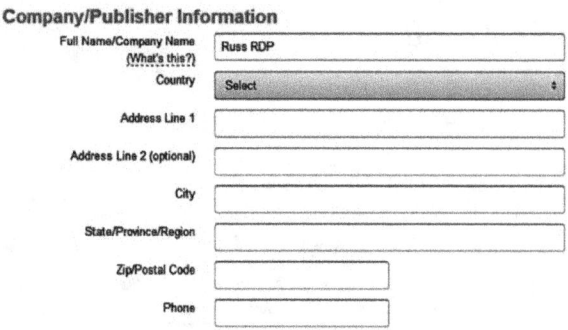

Figure 113 - Company/Publisher Information

a. Enter your **full name/company name**. The company name can be your first and last name.

b. Select your **country** from the drop-down list.

c. Enter your **address.**

d. Then enter your city, your state, postal code, and phone number.

3. Next, you need to enter your **tax information.**

    This takes the form of an online tax interview where you click the button to start and then follow the procedure through. Figure 114 shows the first step of the interview process:

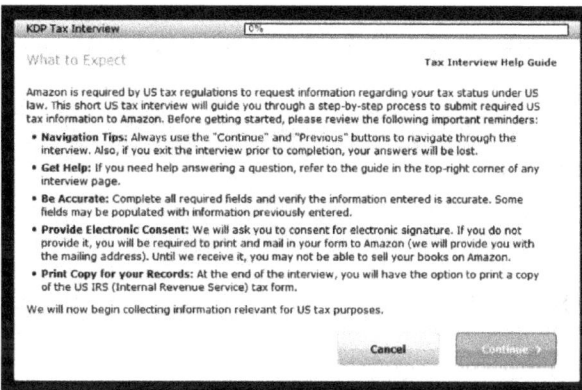

Figure 114 - Start Tax Interview

It's not possible for me to document this entire process due to the number of variables, but the process is straightforward and help is available on each screen.

5.2.1. Add Bank Account

Once complete, you need to enter your bank account details where you will receive your royalty payments:

4. Click on **Add a bank account**.

5. Select the **country** your bank is in.

Figure 115 - Add Bank Account Information

6.   Add your bank account information, ensuring that all fields match your exact bank details.

7.   Click on **Done**.

5.2.2. Add Marketplaces

Next, you can select to add your marketplaces. There is a list of countries available:

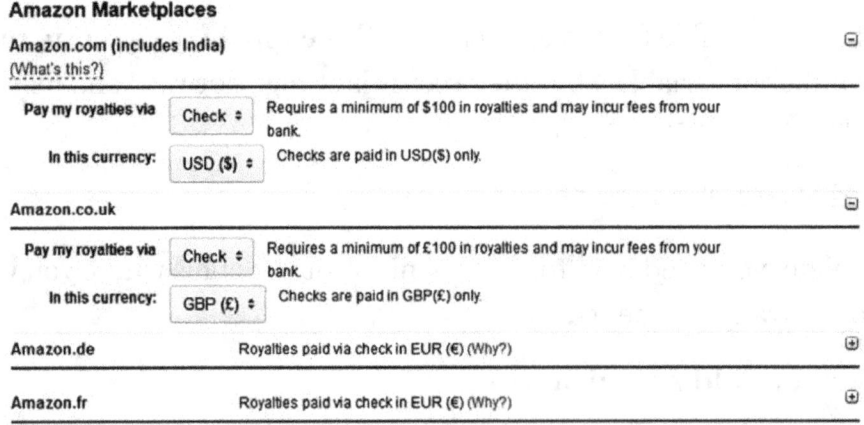

Figure 116 - Amazon Marketplaces

8. Click on any of the marketplaces to reveal further information where you can select how to have your royalties paid by sales in that marketplace, and also the currency from each.

9. Once complete, click on the **Save** button to save all your information.

Your account information is now complete and you can publish your book.

5.3. Add New Title

Click on **Bookshelf** to go back to your homepage within KDP. You will see:

Figure 117 - Welcome to KDP

Adding a new title is a three-step process: **enter your book**, **your rights and pricing**, and **KDP Select Benefits**.

5.3.1. Enter Your Book

To enter your book:

1. Click on the **Start your title now** button.

2. The first thing you will see is **Introducing KDP Select**. I have made a little note about it in Appendix G, but make sure that you read the terms and conditions before you decide what to do.

    Amazon has recently changed the rules regarding payments, and it is quite likely that they will do so again. If you wish to enroll in KDP Select, then check the box:

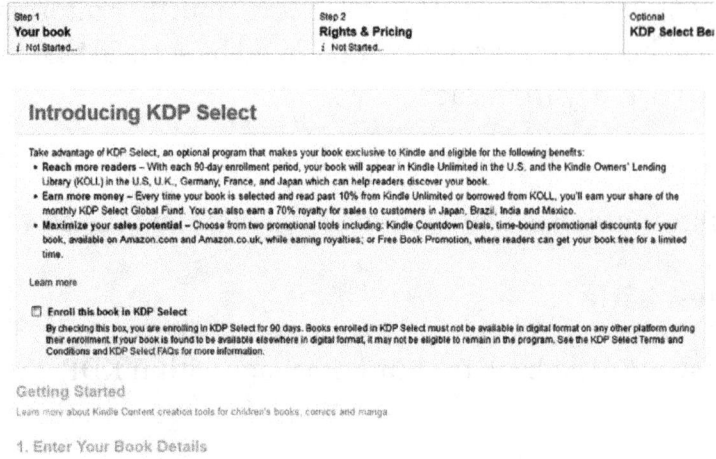

Figure 118 - KDP Select

3.   Next, you need to enter your book details, including: **title, subtitle, edition number, publisher,** description of your book, **book contributors**, **language**, and **ISBN** (if appropriate):

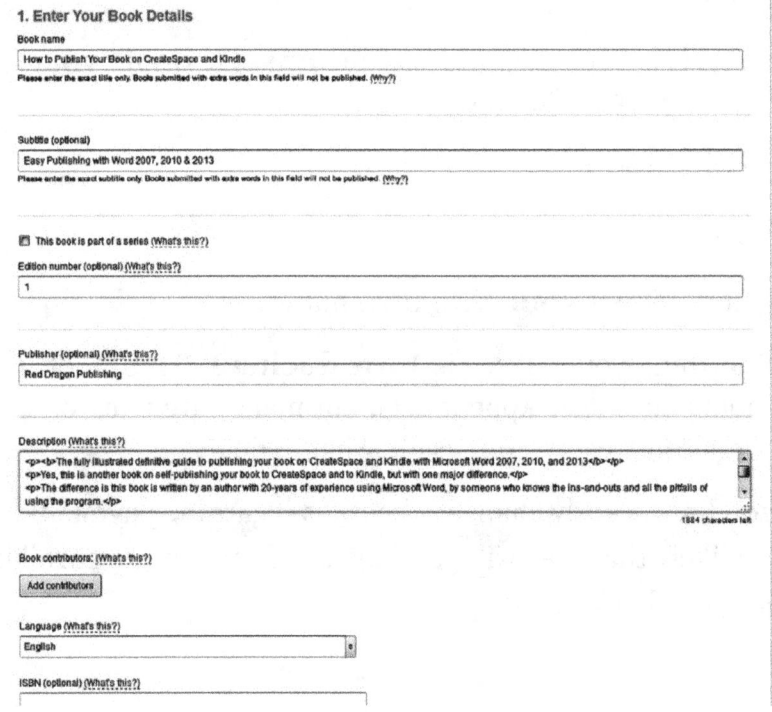

Figure 119 - Book Details

4. I've used the same description from my CreateSpace book for this.

5. You need to click on the **Add Contributors** button to add at least one contributor: bear in mind that the author is not even linked to the book yet, so at the very least you will need to do that.

> If you are writing under a pen name, enter that here.

6. Regardless of whether you have an ISBN number or not, Amazon will assign an Amazon Standard Identification Number (ASIN) to your book for you.

7. Next, you need to select your publishing rights. These are either:

   – This is a public domain work.

   – This is not a public domain work and I hold the necessary publishing rights.

   Select the appropriate choice for your book.

Next, you select the **categories** for your book, the **appropriate age range,** the **U.S. Grade range**, and add **your search keywords.**

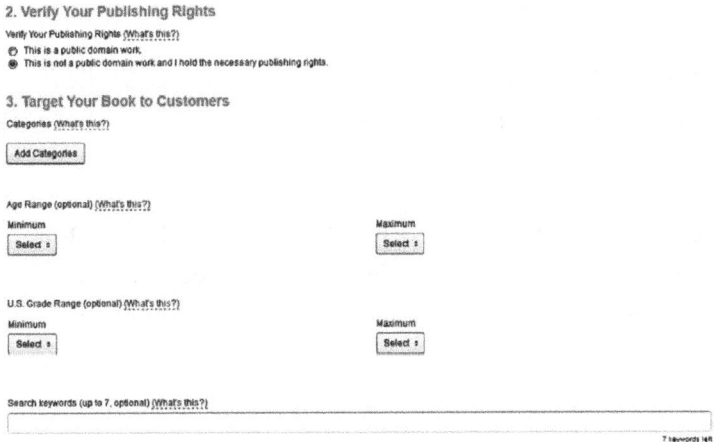

Figure 120 - Target Your Book to Your Customers

Amazon allows you to assign your book to two categories, so:

8.   Click on the **Add Categories** button.

9.   Select the appropriate categories for your book.

Note: you can come back here at any time and change the categories for your book; so, if your sales are down, you can always revisit your book categories and reassign them as required.

If you need to delete a category, click on the small "X" beside it (as shown in Figure 121):

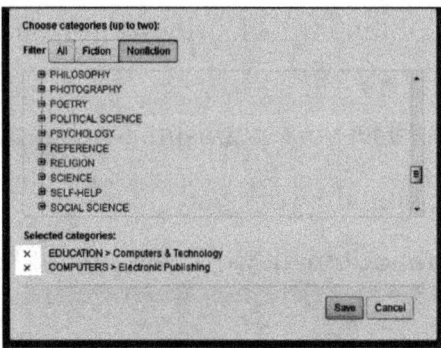

Figure 121 - Delete Category

10.   Once complete, click on **Save.**

11.   Next, you need to specify the **age range** and the **U.S. Grade Range**.

You do not have to specify anything here, but if you do select one option, such as the minimum, you must also select the maximum as well.

12.   Once done, you can then enter your **keywords**. Amazon allows you to specify a maximum of 7; and, as with categories, you can return and modify these as required.

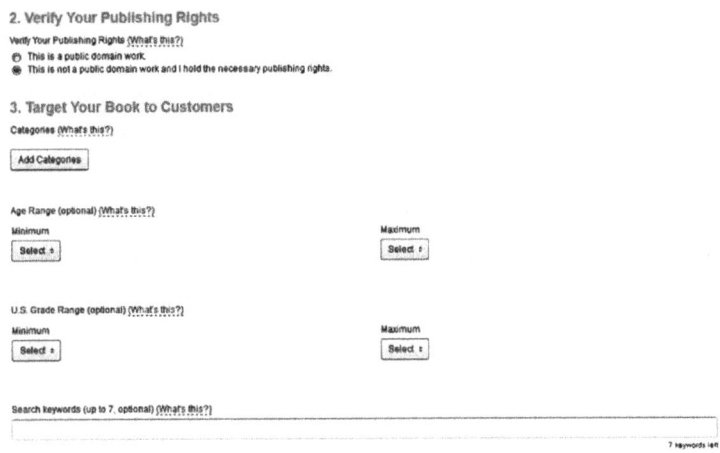

Figure 122 - Customers Targeted

The next steps are to **select your book release option**, **upload or create a book cover**, and then **upload your book file**.

5.3.2. *Compress the Files into a Single Archive*

To compress your files into a zip file:

1. In **Windows Explorer**, select the HTML file **and** the folder.

2. Right-click, select **Send to.**

3. Select **Compressed (zipped) folder**

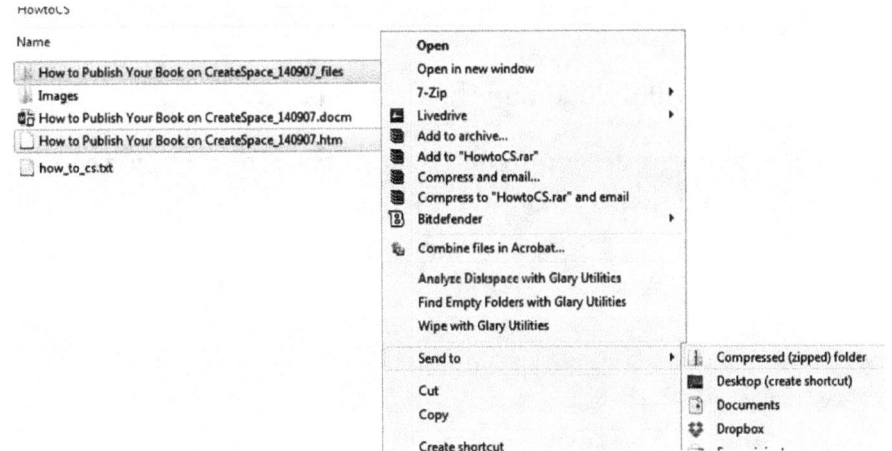

Figure 123 - Compress Files

Bear in mind that Kindle is constantly updating its processes and to get your formatting and layout 100% will require much more tweaking beyond the basic formatting and exporting that Word uses.

For example, with the newer Kindles, it treats indenting and spaces slightly differently. Also, it will replace some of your default settings to what it thinks will suit the device better, and so on.

As it stands now, your Kindle book is 80-85% "there" and, unless you're a perfectionist or know what you're doing with HTML and Kindle, then unless you want to put the time and the effort into squeezing out those last percentages, in the majority of cases, this should easily be good enough.

1. If your book is ready to go, you can select the first option: **I am ready to release my book now**; but, if it isn't, you can select the other option to allow readers to pre-order your book and for it to be delivered automatically when released.

2. Next, you need to upload or create your book cover:

   a. To upload your cover:

      i. Click on the **Browse for image** button

      ii. Navigate to your image and select it.

      iii. Click on **Ok**.

      Your image will upload and the thumbnail will display.

   b. To **use the cover creator**, click on the **Cover Creator** button, the following will display:

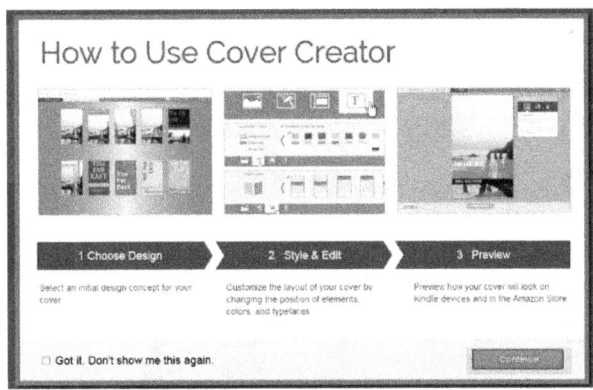

Figure 124 - Kindle Cover Creator

The cover creator is self-explanatory and you can upload your own image(s), or use the sample provided.

Once your cover is uploaded, you can upload your book file.

3. Before you do so, select whether you wish to enable Digital Rights Management (DRM). If you are unsure of what this is, click on the **"What's this"** link to read additional information.

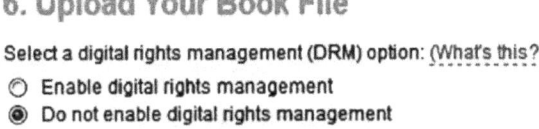

Figure 125 - Digital Rights Management

4. Then you can upload your book file by clicking on the **Browse** button and navigating to and selecting your file.

There are a number of different formats to upload, but the best method is as a mobi or as a zip file.

Once complete, you will see the following:

Figure 126 - Files Uploaded

Then, you can click on the **Preview Book** button to view your book in the online previewer:

Figure 127 - Online Previewer

You can also download the offline previewer as outlined before.

5.   Click on either **Save and Continue** or **Save as Draft**.

You cannot modify your rights and pricing until you save and continue.

5.3.3. *Your Rights and Pricing*

Now, you need to specify the **publishing territories**, **setup your pricing and royalty,** and decide whether to enter your book into the **Kindle Matchbook** and **Kindle Book Lending** offers.

1.   First, you need to select the territories in which you hold rights to the book. You can either leave the default **Worldwide rights – all territories**, or select **Individual territories**.

If you do the latter, then you need to manually select which territories you will allow your book to appear in, and which ones you won't.

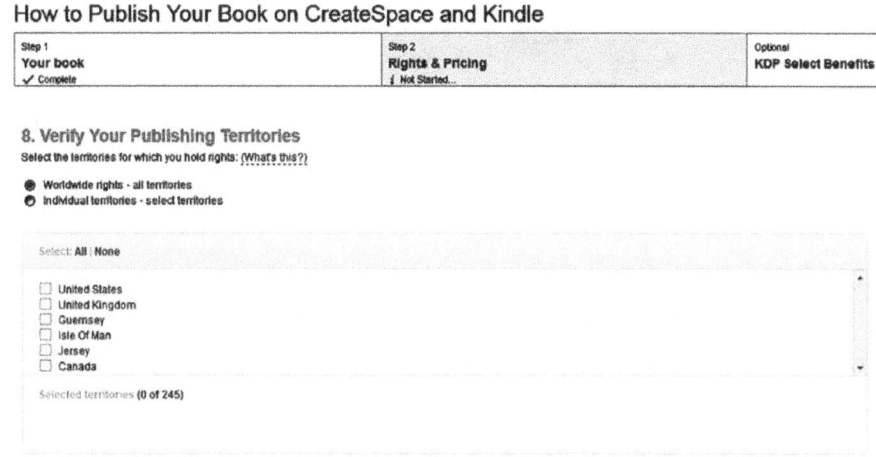

Figure 128 - Verify Publishing Territories

2.   Then, you need to set your royalty option, this will be either 35% or 70%.

Please read up on the differences and the benefits between the two as these will affect your decision. For example, for me and my cheaper Kindle books, I have enrolled them in the 70% scheme as the maximum price allowed is $9.99; yet for our *How to Read Thai* book, it is enrolled in the 35% scheme as its price is higher than that.

3. You then specify your price in the Amazon.com store. All the other stores are set automatically by default, but you can override these on the individual Amazon country site and specify a different price.

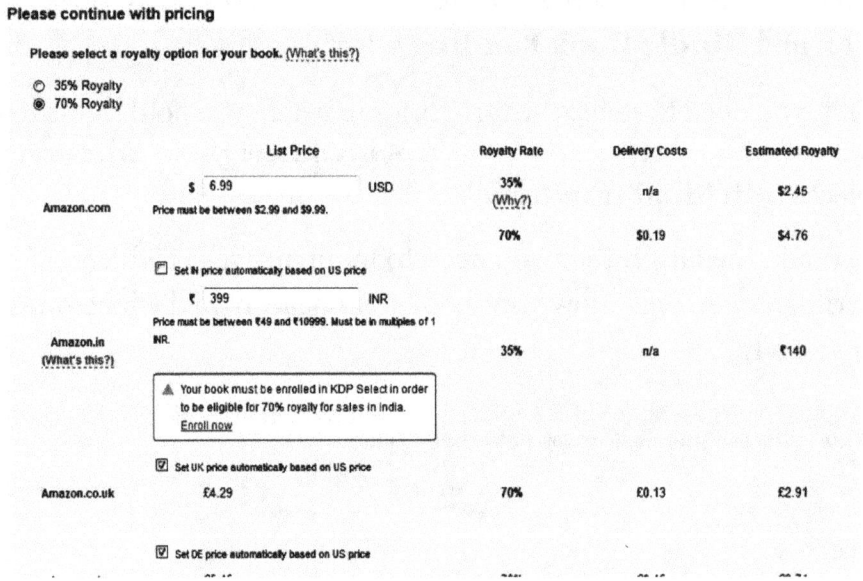

Figure 129 - Pricing Your Kindle Book

4. Next, you can decide whether to enter your book in **Kindle's Matchbook**. This is a feature where you allow a reader who has bought a print copy of your book to purchase the Kindle version for up to $2.99. Check the box to allow it.

    If you do select this box, you can then select a price of either $2.99, $1.99, $0.99, or to allow them to download for free.

Figure 130 - Kindle Matchbook

5.   Next, select whether to allow your book to be enrolled in the **Kindle Book Lending** facility, where users can lend your book to friends and family for up to 14 days.

     If you have selected the 70% royalty option, your book is automatically enrolled in this program.

6.   Finally, you must accept the terms and conditions before clicking on **Save & Publish** or **Save as Draft.**

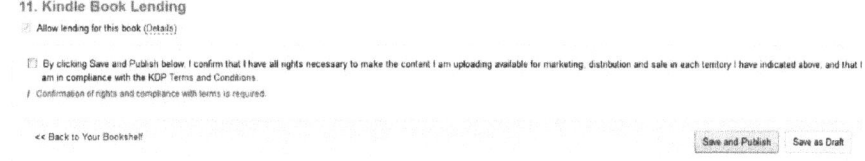

Figure 131 - Kindle Book Lending and Publishing

If you click on **Save & Publish**, your book will be reviewed and will go live on the Amazon Kindle store in approximately 24-hours.

5.3.4. Your KDP Benefits

The KDP benefits sections is optional and consists primarily of **Kindle Select,** a program where you can potentially maximize your audience and earn higher royalties.

Please ensure that you understand the limitations of enrolling in these programs as if you decide to enroll in Kindle Select, your book is restricted solely to Amazon Kindle, and you cannot even give it away on your website.

6. Conclusion

So, that's it. That's your book published on both CreateSpace and Kindle. I hope you enjoyed the journey through this book, and that it wasn't as arduous or tiring as you first thought.

So, that's it. That's your book published on both CreateSpace and Kindle. I hope you enjoyed the journey through this book, and that it wasn't as arduous or tiring as you first thought.

Many people advocate using Word as the basis for publishing to both platforms, and I hope that you can see how easy it can be to use when you understand the way it works and obey some fairly simple rules.

I'm sure you understand that the self-publishing market is constantly changing; and, as such, though correct at the time of going to print, the procedures and graphics in this book are subject to change at any time—unfortunately, that is something over which I have no control.

Having said that, if you do notice any errors then I would really appreciate you letting me know, as I want this book to be useful for years to come and to not only help people to realize their book-writing/publishing dreams, but make it hassle and stress-free too.

If you do like the book and it has helped you, then as reviews on Amazon can literally make or break a book, I'd really appreciate it if you could find the time to leave a review. If you could do it now, that would be great; if you leave it, you'll forget.

Also, and just before I go, I've been doing this for a lot of years now and I wrote this book and created the template to help others realise their dreams. Yes, of course, I want to earn royalties, but that's by-the-by—writing is my job, but it's also my passion and, if this book or the template has helped you in any way, then I'd love to hear from you.

You can email me at russcrowley@red-dragon-publishing.com, and you can also contact me via Facebook: via a send request (Russ Crowley), or via a group I run on writing called *Writing Matters*, where we discuss all things writing, publishing, apps, etc.

I'd love to hear from you and see you over there.

Good luck and I wish you every success with your book.

Russ Crowley, November 2016
russcrowley@red-dragon-publishing.com

Appendices

Appendix A. Interior Options

When you are setting up your book, CreateSpace requires you to select your **interior type, page color**, and **trim sizes**. Though the selection process is extremely easy, some thought needs to be given about your intended audience as if you want to see your book in bookstores, then there are certain sizes which you cannot choose; as such, we'll look at trim sizes first.

Appendix A.1. Trim Sizes

You need to think carefully about the trim size for your book as, not only does this reflect the book size, but it also affects the distribution options available to you. For example, the **Industry standard** book sizes offer the widest distribution to all outlets, whereas the **non-industry standard** sizes cannot be distributed to bookstores or online retailers within the EDC. The sizes and categories are:

Industry Standard Sizes

- 5" x 8"
- 5.06" x 7.81"
- 5.25" x 8"
- 5.5" x 8.5"
- 6" x 9"
- 6.14" x 9.21"
- 6.69" x 9.61"
- 7" x 10"
- 7.44" x 9.69"
- 7.5" x 9.25"
- 8" x 10"
- 8.5" x 11"

Non-industry Standard Sizes

- 8.25" x 6"
- 8.25" x 8.25"
- 8.5" x 8.5"

Appendix A.2. Interior Type

The two options available here are black & white and full-color. The interior type will drastically affect the selling price of your book, as full-color equates to approximately 3-4 times the production price of a black & white book.

For example, we published our 4th book, *How to Read Thai*, as both a black & white **and** as a color book, as though it was ideally meant to be a color book, the "CreateSpace/Amazon" costs for this were astronomical. Of course, we could have simply not bothered, but for optimum learning our system relies heavily on the use of color; and, even though it's just colored text, and despite there not being much color on each page, it is still classed as being a full color book. Let me illustrate this for you...

The B&W version of the book (ISBN: 978-1908203120), with 380-black & white pages, consists of the following (priced at $32.99):

Figure 132 - How to Read Thai (B&W Version)

Its minimum list price is **$16.77**. However, the color version of the book (ISBN: 978-1908203076), with 382-full color pages and, which you will see, we have priced at a much higher **$54.99**, consists of the following:

Figure 133 - How to Read Thai (Color Version)

Due to being classed as full-color, its minimum list price is **$45.99**, almost 3 times the price listing of the black & white book.

Thankfully, Amazon implemented their own discount on the color version, pricing it at around $36 when first released; but, this has been slowly creeping up and is now priced, in January 2016, at its full price.

Appendix A.3. Paper Color

Here you can choose between white or cream, a simple choice with no repercussions anywhere else.

Appendix B. Build Your Cover Online

The CreateSpace online cover creator is a very easy method to use to create your own cover online.

1. To get started, in the **Cover** page of the CreateSpace website, click on the **Build a Cover** Online radio button and, as shown in Figure 134, click on the **Launch Cover Creator** button.

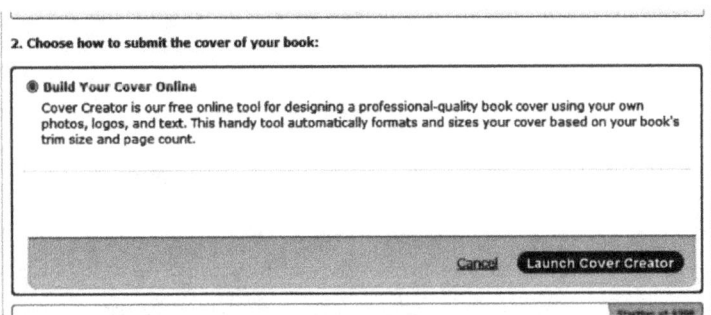

Figure 134 - Build Online Cover Creator

2. The screen will refresh and the **Choose a design** window will display where you can browse and select from five pages of pre-designs.

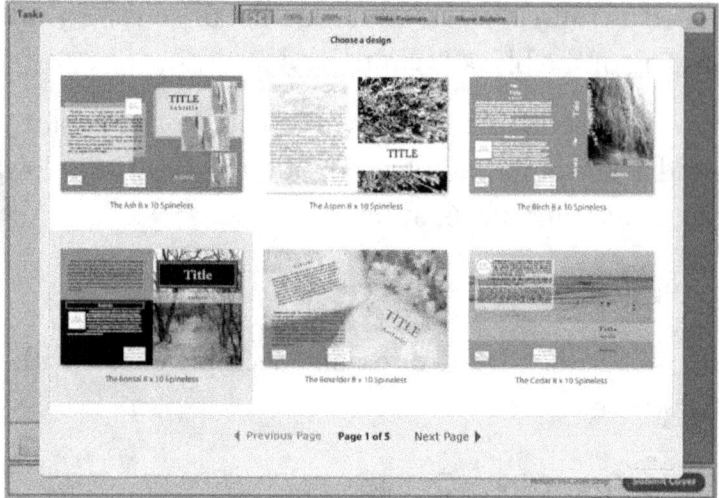

Figure 135 - Choose a Display

3. Once you have selected the design you require, click on the **Ok** button.

4. As shown in Figure 136, I selected the *Boxelder* theme. My title details are already entered.

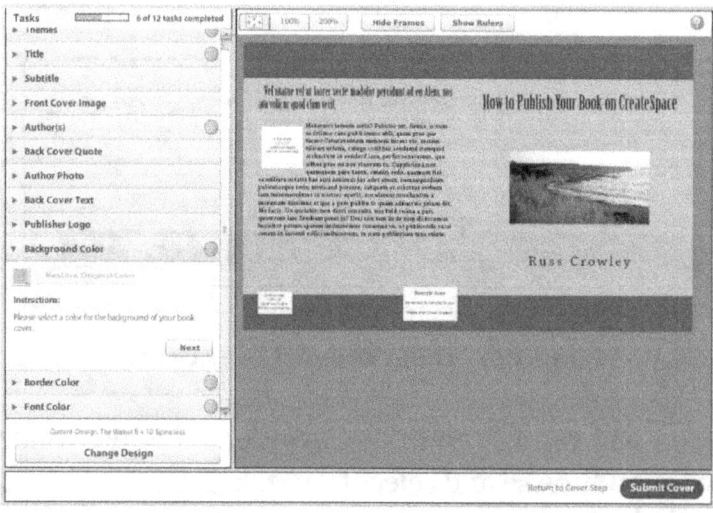

Figure 136 - My Selected Design

5.   You can then modify most areas of your design, including: **Title,
     Subtitle, Front Cover Image, etc.**, and can modify to your heart's
     content.

     If you already have your own image(s), you can upload these in the
     Front Cover Image portion of the editor; and, depending on the
     design selected, additional areas as per your choice.

6.   Alternatively, you can click on the **Use one of our images** button, look
     through and select one of the images from the CreateSpace gallery. To be
     honest, I would not recommend using these because they are: 1) limited;
     and 2), they've probably been used elsewhere multiple times.

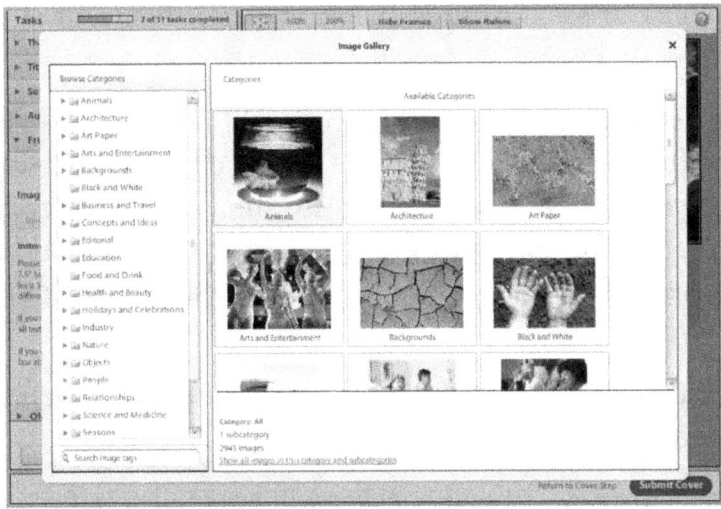

Figure 137 - Image Gallery

     If you select one of the CreateSpace images, a **Use this Image**
     button will appear. lick on it to insert that image into your selected
     design.

There is a lot of scope here and if you have a design flair, you will probably be
able to create a stunning book cover that will draw the eye of people looking
through the bookshelves. However, as this is an area in which I am decidedly
lacking, I resorted to using Fiverr.com and paid extra for the .psd file. I can then
open and modify the design in PhotoShop myself.

Appendix C. Proofreading Best Practices

If you intend proofreading and editing your book yourself, then there's no point in going straight from writing your work to reading it—it just doesn't work like that. For the life of me, I cannot remember the source, but I read somewhere years ago that if you don't notice an error in your writing the 1st time, the chance of you noticing it again the 2nd pass decreases by something like 60%. Then, if you don't notice it on the 3rd pass, the chance drops to less than 10%.

As I said, I cannot remember the source, and the figures might be slightly off, but I can safely say that in over 17 years of proofreading and editing, it is pretty accurate: if you don't get it the first time, unless it's blatantly obvious, the chances are you'll never see it. Unless of course you do some, or all, of the following...

1. **Finish your work first**—your work will be riddled with errors (that's what the draft stage is for), so don't bother checking it before it's finished, it'll just waste unnecessary time. Also, unless you're proficient with the shortcut keys for formatting as you go (refer to section 2.5.3), leave formatting until the very end, as this will waste lots of your time if you do it before you're finished.

2. **Spell-check your work**—don't even consider going past this point until you've run a spell-check on your book.

3. **Use a dictionary**—a spell-checker will only tell you if the word is spelled correctly, not if it's the correct use of the word in that particular context. You're a writer, and there are fewer things worse for a reader than spelling errors or incorrect word use.

4. **Be methodical and use a list**—unless you go for the basic service (refer to Sales & Marketing on page 107), the professionals will always go through their work multiple times: one pass looking for one or two "things," another pass looking for something else, and a further pass looking at spelling, typos, etc. Create your own list so you don't cover old ground.

    In addition, take relevant notes as you go to help you later; and, if you know you're weak with certain words, make a list of those problem words and focus on them as you carefully read your work.

5. **Slow down**—you're not reading for speed, you're reading for accuracy, so slow it down!

6. **Give it a rest**!—a rest means put your work aside for as long as possible and don't look at it. The time not looking at it will hopefully be weeks, but if you're anything like me, it's more likely to be days. However, the longer you leave it, the better the chance of picking up errors.

7. **Concentrate**—it's an important enough task to devote your time and energy to it, free from distractions. So, ensure that the environment is such as to allow you to do this.

8. **Be analytical**—forget the story if you can. Just read the words, the sentences, and the paragraph to ensure correctness, consistency, and flow.

9. **Read your work backwards**—if there is a problem sentence, it can help to read it backwards, focusing on the component words to see if they are correct and make sense.

10. **Check dates, statistics, and facts**—when you've checked them, check them again, against a different source if possible.

11. **Read it on/in a different medium**—I'm fortunate in that I have an iPad and I use the GoodReads app for reading all my work as part of my second edit (my first edit is on the computer after I've written it).

    I will pick up a lot of errors at this point. I will then make those changes and leave the book alone for days/weeks without looking at it again (refer to item 6 in this list).

    For my 3rd edit, I print out a double-sided hard-copy and read it on that medium. It works for me and I always see yet another round of errors.

12. **Read your work out loud**—this is one of the best tips for proofreading as you will read it naturally and any errors in grammar, spelling, or punctuation should become obvious.

13. **Get a friend to help**—see if a friend will read your work for you. If you can get them to read it out loud, it'll be even more useful as this gives you

an alternative point-of-view for your work. People will read naturally and if it sounds weird, perhaps you might want to look at the structure.

Thirteen is a good number to stop on, I hope these tips help you.

Appendix D. eStore Setup and Discount Codes

The main two key aspects of the CreateSpace estore are: 1) you obtain a far better royalty than you do through Amazon or the EDC; and, 2) you can offer discount codes to customers as an incentive to purchase.

As I mentioned in Appendix A.2, when I published the color version of *How to Read Thai*, I neither had any idea that Amazon would discount the book to the level they did, nor did I have any control over this then or since; and, they could raise it to the full price at any time. However, I can (and do) offer discount codes through CreateSpace, and they're easy to setup.

First though, a look at the estore setup.

Appendix D.1. eStore Setup

The estore and discount codes setup facilities are available via the **Channels** section of your project.

1.   Click on the hyperlink to **estore setup**.

2.   The screen will refresh and the following will display:

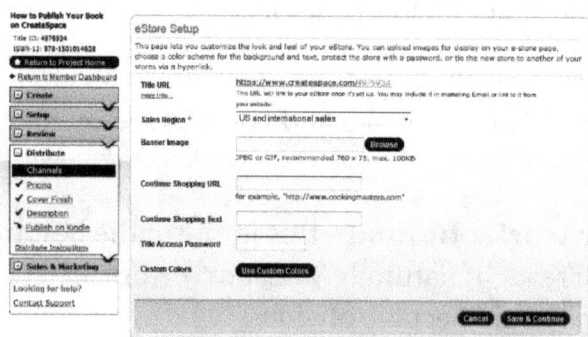

Figure 138 - eStore Setup

The title URL is fixed, but you can now enter the following information:

- **Sales Region**—select the sales region from the drop-down list. This field is compulsory.

- **Banner Image**—you can upload a jpeg or a gif banner image with recommended dimensions of 760 x 75 pixels and a maximum file size of 100kB.

- **Continue Shopping URL**—you can use this URL to send them back to your homepage, e.g. http://www.1clickbookcreation.com

- **Title Access Password**—if you wish, you can protect your CreateSpace estore with a password.

- **Custom Colors**—this option allows you to set your own color scheme for your estore.

Hopefully, all this is self-explanatory, but once you've setup your information, your book's estore page will reflect your chosen selection. Unfortunately, once you click on **Save & Continue**, CreateSpace decides to return you to your Channel's page, so if you haven't already opened your estore page in a new browser window, you'll have to go back in and check it out.

Click on the Title URL link to open your estore page in another tab.

You can now setup your discount codes.

Appendix D.2. Discount Codes

Full instruction for adding a discount code are given on the website's discount code page, but to access this from your book's **Channels** page:

- Click on **Discount codes**. The page will refresh and following will display:

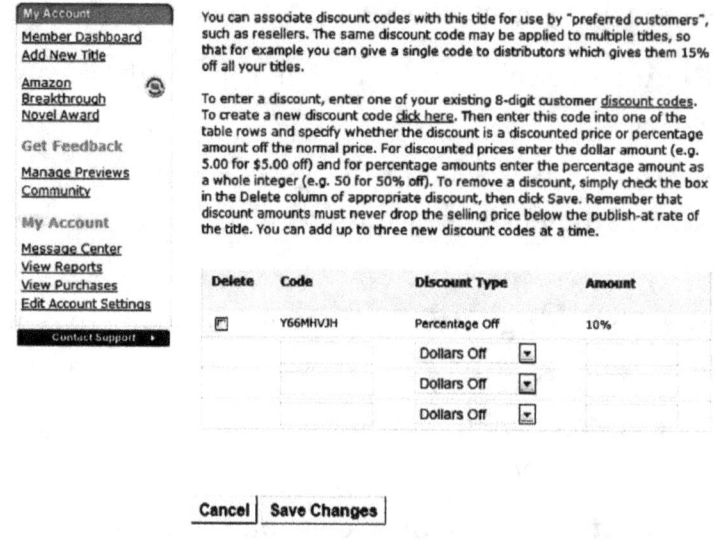

You can associate discount codes with this title for use by "preferred customers", such as resellers. The same discount code may be applied to multiple titles, so that for example you can give a single code to distributors which gives them 15% off all your titles.

To enter a discount, enter one of your existing 8-digit customer discount codes. To create a new discount code click here. Then enter this code into one of the table rows and specify whether the discount is a discounted price or percentage amount off the normal price. For discounted prices enter the dollar amount (e.g. 5.00 for $5.00 off) and for percentage amounts enter the percentage amount as a whole integer (e.g. 50 for 50% off). To remove a discount, simply check the box in the Delete column of appropriate discount, then click Save. Remember that discount amounts must never drop the selling price below the publish-at rate of the title. You can add up to three new discount codes at a time.

Delete	Code	Discount Type	Amount
☑	Y66MHVJH	Percentage Off	10%
		Dollars Off ▼	
		Dollars Off ▼	
		Dollars Off ▼	

Figure 139 - Discount Code Page

As you can see, I've already set one discount code on my book.

To set another discount code:

1.   In the paragraph **above** the table, there is a text hyperlink called **discount codes**, you need to click on this and setup your discount code from there. The page will open in a new tab.

Your Discount Codes
These are your active discount codes

Discount Code	Number of Discounts
2458A8TT	27
AQ6MS6VZ	11
S8J4V9ZZ	185
KSTKEPUT	34
Y66MHVJH	5
XEQ6M6RS	0
6TRB43AP	0

New Code

Figure 140 - Active Discount Codes

CreateSpace allows you to set 8 discount codes for your estore. Once they have been set, you will need to record the code you will apply for the next step.

2.   Close this tab.

3.   In your discount code page, enter the discount code into the next available box.

4.   Select the **discount type** from the drop-down list:

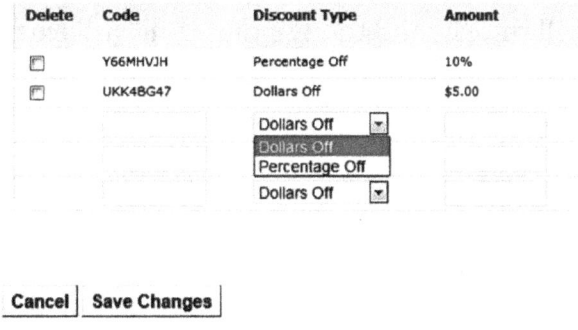

Figure 141 - Discount Type

5.   Then enter the discount amount in the discount box.

6.   Click on **Save Changes**.

Your discount code is now applied, and you can email this to your customers, put it on your website, etc. This discount will only apply to this book. If you have more than one title, you will need to modify the discount codes on a per title basis.

Removing a Discount Code

If you want to remove a discount code, in the discount code:

•   Identify the code you wish to remove.

•   Select the check box in the **Delete** column:

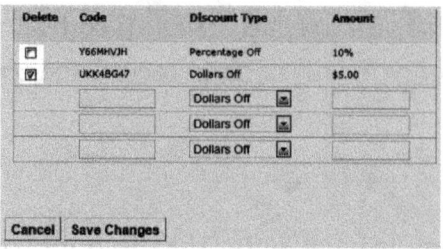

Figure 142 - Delete Discount Code

7.   Click on the **Save Changes** button.

The screen will refresh and though that code still exists, it will no longer be active for this particular title.

If you have applied this code to multiple titles, you will need to remove it from each one manually.

Appendix E.   Tax Information

CreateSpace and Amazon will require your tax information details before you can proceed too far with creating your book; and, most definitely before you'll start receiving royalty payments.

There are too many regulations for them to be covered in this book, but all required information and guidance is available from CreateSpace's website, URL as follows:

https://www.createspace.com/Help/Index.jsp?orgId=00D300000001Sh9&id=5 0170000000k57aAAA

As a non-U.S. national, I was required to fill out and submit their IRS form W-8 by mail. Please ensure you comply, otherwise it's you who will either suffer reduced royalty payments, or even payment suspension.

Appendix F.   Royalty Payments

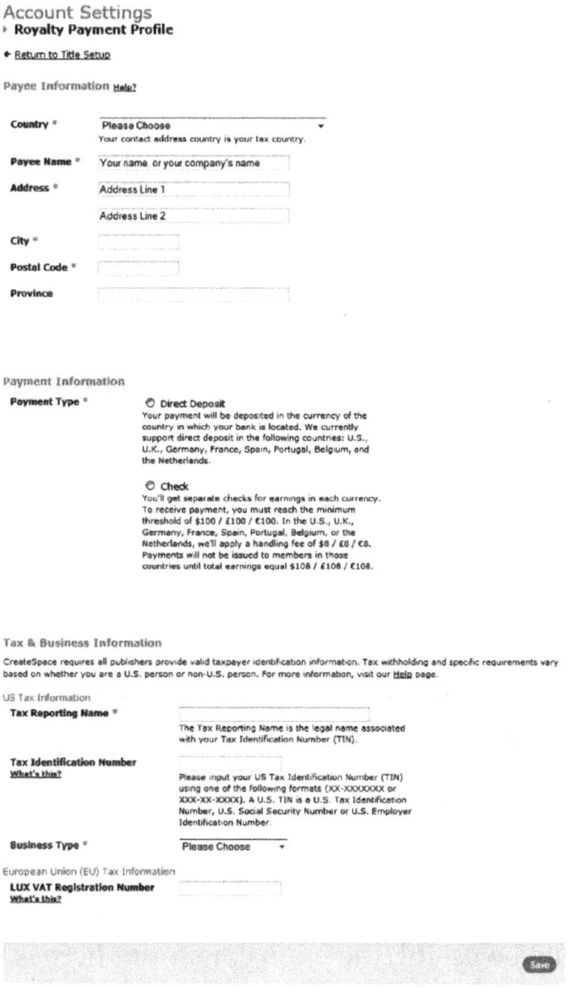

Figure 143 - Royalty Payment Profile

1.   Then, once you've entered all the required information, click on **Save**.

2.   The screen will refresh and your updated **Royalty Payments Information** will display.

Figure 144 - Updated Royalty Payments Profile

3.   Click on **Return to Title Setup**.

Appendix G. KDP Select

KDP can be used to allow people to download your book for free on a maximum of five days in a 90-day period.

This can be a very effective way of gaining access to a wider audience and to generate reviews for your book—essential for any new author.

Please read the requirements for being in KDP Select as though it appears to be something which could be useful, the main constraint here is that while enrolled in the program, your book cannot be offered digitally anywhere else, free or otherwise; and, flouting this rule could land you in trouble with Amazon.

You will be paid for each download of your book if the reader actually reads 10% of it. If they don't, then you will receive nothing.

About the Author

Russ is British and lives in Thailand. He joined the British Army at the age of 19 and, after serving for seven years, left the Armed Forces to work on the gas rigs in the North Sea. In 1994, four years later, Russ suffered an industrial injury which turned his life upside down (literally), and ended his offshore career.

The next few years of rest and rehabilitation were spent learning about computers and, in 1997, he turned his hand to technical authoring.

Apart from a few years of teaching scuba-diving and delivering sailing yachts, Russ has worked as a Technical Author, Technical Editor, author, editor, proof-reader, web-designer, product creator, and other associated tasks full-time.

Happily married to Duangta, they live in the NE of Thailand with their dog, Odi. Together, they've authored/co-authored ten books. Five of which teach English speakers the Thai language (www.learnthaialphabet.com). Russ has a 1st Class Honours degree in English Language.

Russ is also a certified Microsoft Word Expert.

Bibliography

BISG. (2014). *Complete BISAC Subject Headings, 2013 Edition*. Retrieved
    August 30, 2014, from BISG - Book Industry Study Group:
    https://www.bisg.org/complete-bisac-subject-headings-2013-edition

Mansfield, R. (2013). *Mastering VBA for Microsoft Office 2013* (1st ed.). Sybex.

Sedwick, H. (2014). *Self-Publisher's Legal Handbook: The Step-by-Step Guide to
    the Legal Issues of Self-Publishing.* Ten Gallon Press.

Shepard, A. (2014). *From Word to Kindle: Self Publishing Your Kindle Book with
    Microsoft Word, or Tips on Designing and Formatting Your Text So Your
    Ebook Doesn't Look Horrible (Like Everyone Else's).* Shepard Publications.